101 GREATEST
MAGIC SECRETS
EXPOSED

25

BRAINSTORM

***You will be able to identify a card a
member of the audience has mentally chosen.***

T his is a mathematical-type card trick. You can use it as a magic
trick, a mentalism trick, or a small stage trick—on television or as
part of a close-up routine. This is the TV or stage version.

A large blackboard is put on the stage. Attached to it are sixteen playing cards faceup. They are arranged in four rows of four
cards each. Ask a member of the audience (or everyone in the audience) to mentally choose a card. The magician takes the audience through a series of moves and ends up on the chosen card.

THE SECRET:

The cards are laid out from top to bottom as follows: row 1
(horizontal), red, then three black cards; row 2, black, then three
red cards; row 3, black, red, then two black cards; row 4, black,
then three red cards. (You can use any heart or diamond for the red
cards and any spade or club for the black cards.)

R B B B

B R R R

B R B B

B R R R

1. Ask the audience to choose a black card.•
2. Ask them to move to the right or to the left, to the nearest red card.
3. Then ask them to move up or down to the nearest black card.
4. Diagonally move to the nearest red card.
5. Move either down or to the right to the nearest black card.

If you follow these simple steps correctly, you will always end up on the black card in the third row, third card from the left.

To do this trick as a close-up, count out the sixteen cards onto a table, then have someone start by placing a coin on the first card, moving the coin as your instructions are followed. To do this as a mental trick, write down the identity of the final card and slip it into your pocket. When the trick is complete, remove the slip to show your prediction.

No one remembers the movement order, so they will not be able to re-create what you have done.

26

RISING CARD ILLUSION

***Playing cards mysteriously rise and float through
the air in response to commands.***

THE SECRET:

A long thread of thin black silk. The thread is attached wall to
wall over the stage, from one wing to the other. The thread should
be a few inches above head level, so you can walk under it. One
end is simply tied to a large tack or nail; the other end passes
through a screw eye and continues down almost to the floor,
where a fishing weight is tied to it, keeping the thread taut.

You will need to doctor several playing cards, and the larger
the deck the better the view for the audience. So look for a deck of
the extra-large cards that are about three inches by five inches.
Take a few cards and cut triangular tabs, measuring one inch to a
side, and then paste these tabs on other cards near the top edge on
the back of the cards you will ultimately cause to rise and float in
the air. Only the top portion is pasted to the doctored cards, leaving a downward flap with which the card can engage the thread.

The chosen doctored cards are placed faceup on a table. Place
the card case in front of them, and point it toward the audience.
Set a facedown pack of cards on the case. Within this deck are du-
plicates of the doctored cards. Using any of the forces taught to

you in this book, have audience members choose some or all of the doctored cards.

Return the chosen cards back to the deck. Place the deck faceup on the set of doctored cards resting on the table. Pick up the deck and the doctored cards. Hold the deck upright in your left hand, facing the audience.

Stand just behind the thread. Raise your right hand above the deck and call for a card to rise. When none responds, bring your hand down, snap your fingers, and raise the hand again. This time, go higher and engage the thread with your fingers, bringing it down to the pack. This time square the cards and tap them. In so doing, your right thumb works the thread beneath the point of the tab on one of the gimmicked cards. The left hand grips the deck; the right hand goes up and makes another finger snap. Relax pressure on the deck with your left hand and a chosen card sails up out of the deck. Reach up with your right hand, grasp the card out of midair and off the thread, and place it on the face of the pack. One chosen card has floated out of the deck!

You should practice this trick in front of mirrors. The screw eye can be attached to a mirror set up in front of you. As you perform the trick, watch yourself in the mirror and see the trick from the point of view of your audience.

27

CONVERSATIONS WITH MOVIES

Performing a card trick with an actor in a movie scene

*H*ere is an example of how a little card trick can, with enormous and painstaking preparation, be embellished and become a fascinating illusion. In this trick, you combine magic with the movies.

A movie is shown, center stage. At a certain point in the movie, the magician begins a dialogue with the movie's cast members. Within the dialogue, you ask the movie cast member if he would like to see a trick. The screen actor answers affirmatively. You ask for a volunteer from the audience to help you with this trick.

The audience volunteer pulls at random a card from a deck held by the magician. The chosen card, say, the jack of diamonds, is shown to the audience and then is returned to the deck. The audience volunteer then throws the deck against the film screen and into the face of one of the actors.

There, on the screen, while the film is running, the actor pulls the chosen card from his or her pocket: the jack of diamonds.

THE SECRET:

The brilliant part of this illusion is surely the perfect, technical synchronization of the running film with the interaction produced by the onstage magician. However, the decisive trick is merely to have the woman pull from the deck exactly the jack of diamonds. This is not as difficult as it sounds. Any card force or a rigged magic deck will make this possible. Using the Svengali deck will do the trick.

One such method is to hold the deck toward the audience and spread the lower part of the deck with the visible images facing the audience and making the remark, "As you can see, there are many different cards to choose from." Then the magician squares up the deck and asks the woman to choose a card from the top portion of the deck. The top portion of the deck consists only of jacks of diamonds, many jacks of diamonds.

The whole deck is thrown against the screen. The cards fall all over the stage and out of sight. The trick is complete and the magic miracle has taken place

This trick is similar to the Card on the Ceiling (see page 29), in which the chosen card ends up attached to the ceiling. In the second version of that trick, a duplicate of the chosen card is attached to the ceiling before the trick is performed. After the duplicate card has been forced upon the participant, the magician throws the deck up against the ceiling (without any forewarning to the audience). Once everyone looks up, they see the chosen card on the ceiling as the rest of the deck floats downward.

What is needed for this trick is your own home movie. Film someone and work in the rehearsed dialogue. The actor on the screen, the star of your movie, has the chosen card in a pocket.

The script I used was based on a 1950s television series in

which a television crew came to the home of a famous person and interviewed him. The famous person would give a tour of his house and make small talk. I used the same sort of dialogue. I took a camcorder to a friend's house and did an interview of sorts with him. At one point, I asked if he wanted to see a trick. He agreed. Then I picked the woman from the audience. Everything I said during the trick had been scripted. In that manner, the movie dialogue and mine were coordinated.

28

EGG PREDICTION

A hard-boiled egg predicts a chosen card.

A card is chosen by a member of the audience, then replaced in the deck. A hard-boiled egg, which has been sitting on the table, is inspected, then peeled. Written on the egg is the name of the chosen card.

THE SECRET:

The egg has been specially prepared with a solution of alum and vinegar (mix one ounce of alum with a pint of vinegar). Using a small paintbrush dipped in this solution, write the name of the card to be chosen on the eggshell. Once it dries, the solution vanishes from the shell. Boil the egg until it is hard-boiled.

Now, use any of the forces outlined in this book in order to have the spectator choose the card you want him or her to choose. Pick up the egg and show it to the audience. The writing on the eggshell will have vanished, but the name of the chosen card will be clearly written on the egg white inside the shell.

You can use this trick to predict names, dates, ages, or newspaper headlines.

PART TWO

HYPNOTIC HIJINKS: THE DUNNINGER HYPNOTISM ACT

How to Hypnotize
Members of Your Audience

Here, available for the first time in a book, is the complete Joseph Dunninger hypnotism act.

Professor Joseph Dunninger was one of the late great men of magic. His specialties were mind reading and hypnotism. He once claimed he could hypnotize people while they listened to him over the radio. His hypnotism act was not unique, but his personal charisma made him a popular magician.

Although some magicians feel that a hypnosis act can be part of a magic show, I do not agree. Too many people might actually believe that the hypnosis is actually putting people under their control. This is not the case. Hypnotism within the realm of a magic show is not the same as what a clinical hypnotist will do. In one instance, hypnotism is purely for entertainment while the other has the purpose of healing.

Hypnotic Experiments

The entire purpose of the hypnosis act is to get at least one person to be in a hypnotic trance for the purpose of the hypnotic experiments.

In most cases it is a good idea to have ten to twenty people called up from the audience when you begin with method one. As you continue through to method eight, you will slowly narrow down the group to one or two people. These people will be the ones who really want to be onstage. They are the ones who will most likely play along with the experiments.

As the methods are being perpetrated on the group from the audience, the magician will see who wants to be part of the act and who does not. Keep in mind that some people who come up onstage do so for the sole purpose of making the magician look like a fool. Once you have your final one or two, you can begin the experiments.

The following methods are used to hypnotize people. There are many methods because not everyone will be hypnotized by the same method. The idea is to have several people from the audience onstage with you. Begin with the first method; those who are hypnotized will remain in that state as you move on to the next method, and so on.

In the end, you will have hypnotized the majority of the people onstage. Those who are still not hypnotized should be asked to leave the stage and return to their seats.

Here, then, from the alleged secret notes of the great magician, is the Dunninger Hypnotism Act.

29

Inducing Hypnosis— Method One

*S*tand the subject before you and gaze intently into his or her eyes. Keep your gaze steady and force him or her to look steadily at your eyes. Raise your right hand to a level with his or her ears and pass the hand slowly from the top of the subject's ear to the base of his or her brain, slowly but firmly instructing, "You are becoming tired. Your eyes refuse to waver. You cannot take them from my eyes. Your mind is clear. You must think of nothing but what I am going to command you to do. Your eyelids are tired; now they are fluttering. Your limbs are feeling numb. You are growing increasingly drowsy. You are falling asleep. Sleep, sleep!"

This procedure is continued for a moment or two and somnambulism is usually induced. Keep your eyes on your subject's eyes. Even when you see his or her eyelids flutter, do not remove your eyes from your subject's. Continue speaking in a soothing voice to suggest sleep.

If this method works, move on to the experiment section. If it does not work, move on to method two.

30

INDUCING HYPNOSIS— METHOD TWO

*S*eat the subject in a chair and instruct her or him to completely relax all muscles. Tell her or him to place one hand on top of your thumb. Use your left hand. Have the subject relax and use your thumb as a sort of prop to hold the subject's hand. Gaze intently into her or his eyes, and tell the subject that she or he is about to fall into a calm, peaceful sleep. Suggest she or he is very tired and in need of sleep.

Continue in a monotone voice and suggest that sleep is needed. Then, suddenly pull your thumb away. If the hand falls like a dead weight to the subject's side or into her or his lap, immediately follow it up with these suggestions: "You are sleepy. Very tired. You are to clear your mind of all thoughts. Sleep is what you need. You will soon sleep, sleep!"

Under no circumstances mention hypnotism. Just instruct the subject to relax all muscles, and say that she or he will feel refreshed and clearer minded if your instructions are followed.

If this method works, move on to the experiment section. If it does not work, move on to method three.

31

Inducing Hypnosis— Method Three

Seat the subject and tell him or her to gaze intently at your fore-finger, which you hold a few inches above the subject's eyes, about six inches from his or her forehead. Tell the subject to watch it intently. Rotate the finger in a circular manner for a few minutes while speaking in a firm monotone: "Your eyes are growing heavy. Your eyelids are about to close. Your eyelids feel moist. You cannot see. Your eyes are beginning to wink, they are growing steadily weaker." Repeat this several times if needed and suddenly command the subject to "Close your eyes! Go to sleep!"

Immediately place your fingers on the sides of the subject's head, your thumbs on the forehead just above the eyes. Now move the thumbs outward toward the sides of the temples and make a rotating movement slowly but firmly. Instruct the subject to sleep. Place your thumb at the root of your subject's nose, fingers resting on top of his or her head. Make a downward pass from the back of the subject's head (top of head) to the base of the brain area, employing a firm pressure, all the while continuing in monotone the suggestions that he or she is going to sleep.

If this method works, move on to the experiment section. If it does not work, move on to method four.

32

INDUCING HYPNOSIS— METHOD FOUR

A bright, polished object is held steadily between the thumb and forefinger about six inches in front of the seated subject's eyes at an angle of about 45 degrees above the eyes. This will force the subject to turn her or his eyes upward while steadily concentrating her or his gaze on the object in question.

This steady gaze should cause the subject to become drowsy due to the strain on the eyes in having to gaze upward at the angle mentioned. The light reflecting on the shiny object will soon tire the eyes, causing them to flutter downward, as if to close completely. The hypnotist, watching this, takes advantage of the fact and firmly suggests sleep. As soon as the weary lids begin to close, sharply comes the command, "Open your eyes! You cannot close them. Open wide."

With this, you should have succeeded. If not, move on to method five.

33

INDUCING HYPNOSIS—
METHOD FIVE

*S*eat the subject before you in a chair. Have him or her relax comfortably. Take both of the subject's hands in yours. You should be seated opposite the subject. Take the subject's right hand in your left and with your right hand take his or her left hand. Gently yet firmly tell the subject they are about to give themselves over to sleep. Continue to say that they must go to sleep repeatedly in a monotonous tone of voice. While you are verbally suggesting sleep, gently but firmly draw your thumbs back and forth along the subject's hands. Continue to repeat instructions of sleep while you continue stroking the hands.

Still not hypnotized? Then move on to method six.

34

INDUCING HYPNOSIS— METHOD SIX

*P*lace a single spot (ace of diamonds or hearts) on a wall about 30 degrees or so above the line of the subject's vision. Tell the subject to gaze intently upon the pip on the card and completely relax,

all the while concentrating on sleep. "Clear your mind of all other thoughts," you should say.

As the subject gazes at the card, slowly draw her or him back away from the wall, slowly, step by step, all the while saying that she or he will be asleep soon.

Have one of your assistants place a chair behind the subject, and speak to her or him as follows: "Keep your eyes on that card before you. Think of sleep and only sleep. You are becoming drowsy and I am going to allow you to sit down, as your feet are growing too tired to hold you. Keep your eyes concentrated on the card on the wall." Continue this dialogue as you assist the subject into the chair.

Still not hypnotized? Then move on to method seven.

35

Inducing Hypnosis— Method Seven

*S*tand the subject in front of you; instruct him or her to gaze steadily into your eyes, not between them. Slowly command the subject to clear his or her mind of all thought except that of falling into a deep sleep.

Lightly make passes on both sides of the temples with both your hands, all the while telling the subject to place himself or herself completely under your control: "You are feeling drowsy. . . ."

Continue with the passes, now and then lightly touching the subject between the eyes. Slowly withdraw your hands to the front of the subject, on a line with his or her armpits. Command the subject to sway toward you, then back again. Continue this for a short time, and then continue with your commands, always made in a firm monotone voice.

If this method works, move on to the experiment section; if it does not work, move on to method eight.

36

Inducing Hypnosis— Method Eight

*T*his method is very useful in hypnotizing a person who finds it difficult to concentrate upon the one idea of sleep. The failure to concentrate is caused by a confusion of ideas in the mind of the subject and at times proves confusing to the hypnotist.

After seating the subject in a comfortable position, explain that you want him or her to go to sleep, then request him or her to become perfectly passive and to look directly at you. In a slow, monotonous, and firm manner, begin to count. Instruct the subject that on each count he or she should close his or her eyes and open them between the counts.

The hypnotist continues to count fairly slowly up to forty or fifty, though if this counting is properly done, many subjects will be unable to open their eyes by the time fourteen or fifteen has been reached.

Should this be the case, continue to count monotonously a while longer. The subject will, as you continue to count, try to raise his or her eyelids, apparently thinking that he or she is continuing to open and close the eyes. When the subject's head begins to droop and he or she acts very drowsy, discontinue counting and continue to speak to the subject, saying that he or she is very tired and is slowly, but surely, beginning to fall asleep.

By this time, the subject will be ready to move on to the experiment part of the act.

37

HYPNOSIS EXPERIMENT NUMBER ONE

The falling backward test

*T*he subject stands erect with hands hanging relaxed at the sides. The head inclines slightly backward, and the subject gazes upward at an angle of about 45 degrees. The hypnotist holds his clenched fists at the base of the subject's brain. The subject is then commanded to concentrate his mind on the idea of falling backward, although he or she must make no physical effort to do this.

The hypnotist then places his left hand over the forehead and eyes of the subject and says, "I want you to concentrate upon falling backward; you will soon feel a desire to fall backward. Yield to that impulse. I will catch you as you fall. Do not be afraid; concentrate on falling backward."

As the hypnotist removes his hands, the subject is seen swaying slowly backward then forward, then fall backward into the waiting arms of the assistant.

38

HYPNOSIS EXPERIMENT NUMBER TWO

Hand-clasping test

*C*hoose one of the subjects who has successfully carried out your instructions in the earlier portion of the hypnotic act and ask him or her to relax all the muscles of his or her body. Tell the subject to rest and clear his or her mind. In a firm voice, the magician says, "Stand up, please. Thank you. Fold your hands in front of you. Do not lock them tightly, but easily. Now, follow my instructions to the letter. Tighten up the clasp of your hands. So! Now make your arms as rigid as you can. Stiffen them up, please. More, more! That is it. Now, bear in mind this thought: You cannot get your hands apart. You are unable to unclasp them until I command you to do so!" The magician now squeezes the subject's hands together tightly.

Repeat over and over that the subject's hands cannot be taken apart. After a bit of byplay, during which the subject is unable to pull his or her hands apart, the hypnotist sharply claps his own hands together and commands the subject to "Awaken!" At this point, the subject's hands can be separated.

39

HYPNOSIS EXPERIMENT NUMBER THREE

The falling forward test

*T*he subject stands erect with hands hanging relaxed at the sides. The head inclines slightly forward, and the subject gazes downward at an angle of about 45 degrees. The hypnotist holds his clenched fists at the base of the subject's brain. The subject is then commanded to concentrate on the idea of falling forward, although he or she must make no physical effort to do this.

The hypnotist then places his left hand over the forehead and eyes of the subject and says, "I want you to concentrate upon falling forward; you will soon feel a desire to fall forward. Yield to that impulse. I will catch you as you fall. Do not be afraid; concentrate on falling forward."

As the hypnotist removes his hands, the subject sways slowly backward then forward, then falls forward into the waiting arms of the assistant.

PART THREE

ROPE AND
KNOT TRICKS

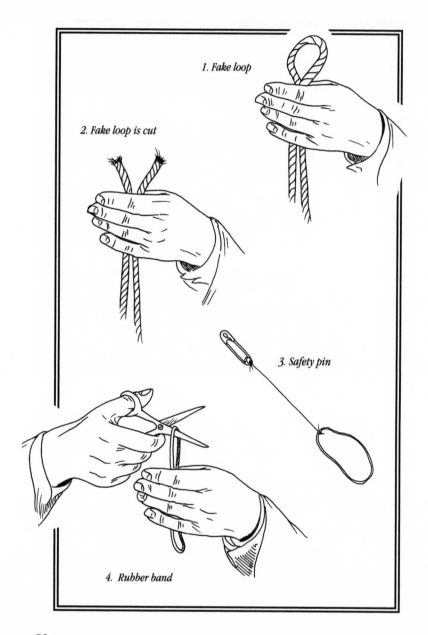

1. Fake loop

2. Fake loop is cut

3. Safety pin

4. Rubber band

40

Cut and Restored Rope—Modern Version

A rope is cut in two, then restored

A member of the audience examines a rope. The magician forms a loop with the rope, hands a pair of scissors to a member of the audience and asks this person to cut the rope. The rope is magically restored by the magician, who then hands it out for further examination.

The props:

A rope around five feet long, a safety pin, a rubber band, and a pair of scissors.

The secret:

Cut about six inches off the five-foot rope, make a loop, and tie a knot in it. Cut the rubber band. On one end of the rubber band, attach the safety pin; on the other, attach the rope loop (3).

Fasten the safety pin inside your sleeve (4). The loop should extend down to your wrist.

Hand the rope out to be examined. While it is being examined, casually pull the loop down from your wrist into your hand. Once the rope has been handed back to you, loop this rope. As you pull the loop out (1), it is the loop on the elastic you pull above your hand. Cut this loop (2). It now appears that the rope has been cut into two pieces. Actually, you have not cut the rope, which was examined; you have only cut the loop, which is attached to the rubber band.

Continue cutting the small loop of rope until very little remains. Bunch up the long rope in your hand and announce that you will magically restore the rope. Say a magic word, then show that the rope is whole again. Hand the rope back out for examination. In the meanwhile, allow the rubber band to yank any remaining part of the small loop back up your sleeve.

41

CUT AND RESTORED STRING—WITH KEY

A cut string is restored without any sign of damage.

A key hangs from a tied loop of string. The magician cuts the string. After showing that the ends are cut, the magician ties these ends together. Now the string contains two tied knots. The magician cuts the string again; this time he cuts a knot off the string. The string is untied and it is seen to be whole.

THE SECRET:

Cut two inches off a ten-inch string. The type of string used in bakeries works well for this trick. String a key (1) onto the balance of the ten-inch string (now eight inches long). With a dab of glue, attach the cut ends of the eight-inch string. On the opposite of the glued ends, tie the two-inch string. When the glue is dry, it appears that the key is on a knotted string.

When presenting this trick, show the key on the string. With a scissors, cut the glued ends (2). Then cut the fake knot off (3). Tie the glued ends together and you have accomplished a miracle (4). The string has been cut, then magically restored to a string with a single knot in it.

42

VANISHING KNOT

How to tie a knot that is not a knot

A magician ties a single knot in a handkerchief and places the handkerchief on a chair. Then the magician lifts the handkerchief again and the knot has disappeared (this trick is usually the preliminary for the floating hanky).

THE SECRET:

A false knot tie. Hold one end of the hanky in each hand (let's call the end in your left hand A and the one in your right hand B). Hold end A of the handkerchief between the first and second fingers of the left hand and end B in your right hand. Curl the third and fourth fingers of the left hand down to grasp the handkerchief securely. Bring end B into the right hand over these fingers and in front of the first and second fingers. Grip B between thumb and base of first finger, releasing your right hand.

With the right hand, reach inside the loop of the handkerchief and grasp B. End B of the handkerchief is held tightly between the second and third fingers of your left hand as well as the thumb and first finger of the left hand. Bring A down and through loop of the handkerchief. As you continue to pull end A to the right, curve your second and third fingers and draw them backward a little, pulling part of the handkerchief with them. This causes a looping of the handkerchief that looks like a real knot.

Release the second and third fingers from the knot and hold the handkerchief as if you have completed the knot. Lay the handkerchief on the seat of a chair or on a table. Then pick up end B with a slight upward jerk and the knot fades away. If desired, instead of placing the hanky down, merely pull both ends of it and it unties as you hold it between your hands.

Experience will teach you how tight or how loose to make your knot. It must be tight enough to hold and yet loose enough to untie easily. This is a pretty effect when worked with two or three brightly colored silks. Tie each one with a knot, and then tie their ends together, forming a chain of silks. Place them down on a table. With a quick upward jerking motion, snap them up off the table. All the knots will dissolve at the same time.

43

THE KNOT IN THE MIDDLE

The rope that ties its own knot

*T*he magician holds a length of rope with one end in each hand. He invites a spectator to do the same with another piece of rope. Stating that it would be impossible to tie a knot in a rope without letting go of one end, the magician proceeds to drape the rope over his arm, forming a series of simple loops and twists. This is done slowly, without letting go of the ends, so the spectator can copy every move the magician makes with his rope. Still holding both ends, the magician shakes the rope from his arm— a knot appears, magically, in the center. No knot is formed in the spectator's rope, although he is sure he has copied the magician's every move.

David Copperfield says: "Tricks of the 'Do As I Do' type are always effective, and this is one of the best. With a little practice and one simple, secret move, you can baffle your audience time after time." I appreciate David's kind words. When I first developed this trick, the magic community did not consider it much of a trick. Now, owing to David, it is considered a trick that he calls "one of the best."

THE SECRET:

You need two ropes (strings, shoelaces, etc.), each about four feet in length, one for yourself, the other for a spectator.

1. Hold your rope near the ends between the thumb and index finger of each hand, with the rope hanging down between them.

2. Bring your right hand inward (toward you) and drape the rope over your left wrist.

3. Draw the right end of the rope downward and beneath the hanging loop. This divides the hanging loop into two sections, left and right.

4. Insert your right hand (still holding the right end) through the left section of the loop and, in the same continuous action (without letting go), bring your hand back through the right section of the loop, nipping the rope at Point A as shown. Another way to describe Step 4 is that your right hand, still holding its end, goes into the loop and picks up Point A on the back of your right loop and picks up Point A on the back of your right wrist. Point A is then pulled out through the loop to form the setup in Step

5. Without releasing either hand, move your right hand back to the right, bringing the nipped rope with it. Point A is now resting on the back of your right wrist. (*Note:* This is the only part of this excellent magical puzzle that is difficult to illustrate. Try it with the rope in your hands. Sometimes doing rather than reading helps brings the specific steps to life.)

6. Move your right hand level with your left, and pull the rope taut so it forms the crisscross pattern between your wrists as shown. Note that in the illustration a new spot is indicated on the rope, Point B. Point B is just below the end held by the right hand. Now relax the tension on the rope and tilt both hands forward and downward, so the outside loops, which are pressed against your wrist, begin to slide over the ends of your hands.

7. You are now ready for the secret move. As the rope begins to fall off your wrists, your right hand prepares to secretly release its end and grasp the rope at Point B as described in Step 8.

8. As the loops slide completely over and off your hands, draw your hands apart. At the same time, release the right end of the rope with your thumb and index finger, and secretly grasp Point B with your other three fingers. Because of the tossing movement of the loops as they fall off your wrists, the audience is completely unaware of this small move. This is the whole secret of the trick. Since you did let go of the end for a moment, a knot can be formed.

9. As you draw your hands apart, the right end of the rope will automatically pull through the little loop, forming a knot in the center of the rope.

10. Your right thumb and index finger immediately regain their original grip on the end of the rope, so it all looks the same as the knot is formed.

Additional advice: All through the routine, you should emphasize that you never release the ends of the rope. Yet a knot still appears in the rope. That makes this an impossible knot. Practice the moves until they become smooth and natural.

When you present the effects, do each move very slowly and systematically, so the spectators can follow them easily. Your purpose is to show the audience exactly how to do it—except for the final toss, where you secretly release the right end of the rope, enabling you to produce a knot where everyone else fails. Although the spectators copy your moves with ropes of their own, they will always miss the vital point, making the trick more baffling each time it is repeated.

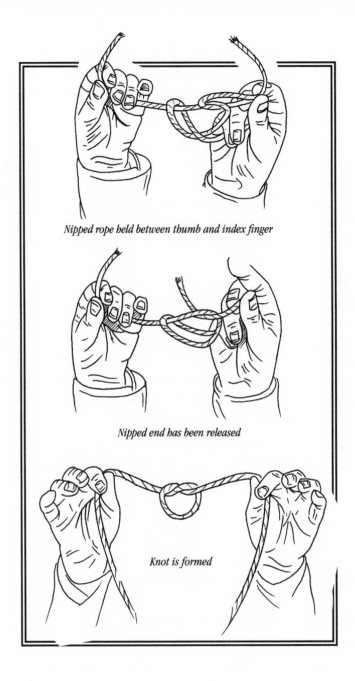

Nipped rope held between thumb and index finger

Nipped end has been released

Knot is formed

When your spectator gets to Step 6, have him or her stop right there and exclaim, Yes, that is it. At that moment take hold of the ends of his or her rope and remove it from his or her hands. The rope will have a knot in the middle. The spectator has done the trick, but does not know how. If the spectator were to continue to the next step, there would be no knot since the next step would need to be the secret move. So why is there a knot for the magician? Because removing the rope from the spectator produces the same effect as the secret move. Try it.

If a ring were left dangling on the rope before doing this trick, it would actually end up in the middle of the knot. I sometimes added this effect to the trick. This is a great trick, if I must say so myself. If you are doing a large stage show or even a television show, have each member of the audience equipped with a length of rope as they enter the show. Then perform the trick and have each member of the audience try along with you. Each person gets to be an assistant and gets to participate in the magic. Rope is cheap, and you can use up fifteen or twenty minutes with this trick. (Since you are paid for your time, this is a good use of it!)

44

HANGMAN

The magician survives a hanging and escapes from the noose.

The magician is led to a large gallows. A rope is put around the magician's neck and his hands are handcuffed. A large timer controls the opening of the trapdoor below the feet of the magician. The magician must get the handcuffs off and get out of the hangman's noose before the timer opens the trapdoor, hanging the magician. However, the timer goes off too soon, the trapdoor opens, and the magician is hung.

For a moment or two, the magician hangs lifeless from the rope. Then slowly the magician begins to move, the escape from the handcuffs is completed, and the magician reaches up and pulls his or her neck out of the noose and jumps down to the stage.

THE SECRET:

The magician is wearing a special harness that hooks into a wire attached to the hangman's noose. There is no chance of injury to the magician. When the noose is slipped over the magician's neck, the harness is secretly hooked to the wire. The noose, which is put around the neck, is real enough, except for one thing: it has been cut in two. Within the two cut ends are magnets holding the noose together. Even if the wire did not hold, the magnets would open and no real harm would come to the magician.

The harness is worn around the body of the magician under his or her clothes. The main support comes from under the arms. The wire is connected directly to the gallows crossbar and runs down through the rope, ending just inside the hangman's noose. A clip is located at the end of the wire for quick hookup and quick release.

The handcuffs can be real or faked. The audience will not be offered the handcuffs, the rope, or the gallows for verification of authenticity. Those who are chosen from the audience to do the hanging hookup and the checking are "plants" (plants are people hired by the magician to act as audience members).

You can have several pairs of handcuffs put on your wrists for effect. The timer is just a large clocklike instrument and it does not actually control the trapdoor. The trapdoor is opened by an offstage assistant by remote control. When the clock misfires, exploding and sparking, it is done for effect. Once the trapdoor opens, the magician will spin just a bit from the force of the fall.

Once free, the magician grabs the rope and hits the release on the wire clip. Then he or she drops to the ground once the magnets in the rope have been separated.

This is a good trick for big arenas such as Madison Square Garden. Nevertheless, it must be built and tested by a professional. No hanging in backyards, please.

45

Ten Thousand Feet of Rope

Escaping from several thousand feet of rope

*A*nother escape trick, which uses an awful lot of rope. Although ten thousand feet is not required, you might try using one hundred feet. The trick starts off with a joke: "I will now be tied up with ten thousand feet of rope!" Well, no one will be fooled when the audience sees the amount of rope and realizes that it is far less than ten thousand feet.

Ask several of the largest, strongest people in the audience to step forward. Give the ends of the rope to two of the individuals and the center to the others. They are then told to tie you up tightly, using every inch of the rope. A giant clock will keep track of their time. Your challenge is to get out of the rope in less time than it took them to tie you up. If you fail? A $10,000 reward is to be paid out to them (or use some other exciting reward for your failure). The idea is to turn this escape into a challenge for the spectators, providing an incentive for them to do a good job of tying you up.

THE SECRET:

"Too many cooks in the kitchen" was something my mother would say when all of us kids tried to do something in the kitchen and eventually nothing would get done. So here, having three or more people trying to tie you up with one long rope will cause them to do a rotten job. Just make sure they do not put the rope around your neck.

Struggle and strain, move and groove as they work to tie you up. When they are finished, the ropes will simply fall off. In most cases, you will be holding the ropes in place. The rope will only be tight at the ends, usually at your hands and feet.

Do not let the ropes off too quickly. Play around a bit and pretend to be stuck. You will get out.

This is a good trick for outdoor presentations. It is inexpensive and packs very small. Always have your assistants nearby, helping to make certain nothing will go wrong.

46

Instant Pole Escape

Instantly escape after you have been tied to a pole

A pole is set in a base that stands in the center of the stage. The magician is tied, head to toe, up against the pole. In a flash, right before the audience's eyes, the escape is made, as the rope falls to the floor.

The secret:

The rope is held in place with a peg. The magician stands with his back to the pole. Unknown to the audience, there is a small loose peg near the center of and in the back of the pole. The rope is wrapped as a continuous loop from the feet up to the peg, then around the peg and up over the top half of the magician.

The rope is tight enough, but the peg is the axis point for the rope. Remove the peg and the rope will loosen and fall.

This trick can be used simply as an escape, or as part of a bigger trick. For example, the magician can be tied in this manner and a screen brought all around him. As other things happen onstage, the magician can escape, then go out through a back door and appear elsewhere in the act. Use your imagination when it comes to combining tricks. This is an example of how you can make a trick better and more than what it is.

47

NOT-SO-GREAT ESCAPE

After being tied up by a volunteer, the magician is able to escape at the blink of an eye.

THE PROP:

A forty-inch-long cotton rope.

THE SECRET:

Tie a simple knot in the rope, forming a loop. Put your left hand into the loop and have a volunteer pull the ends, thus trapping your hand in a knot. As he does so reach down and grab the left end of the rope between the thumb and forefinger of your left hand. Turn around and put your hands together behind your back, enabling your right hand to get under the piece of rope you had in your left hand.

Have the volunteer tie the rope over your right hand as well. The loop you made with your left hand is, in fact, the slack you need to get your hands out of the bond. With a slight twist of your hands, you are able to take your hands out of the bonds and put them back to have the volunteer check the knots. The best part is that you are able to get both hands out of the bondage within seconds.

48

Cut and Restored Rope

The magician cuts a rope and puts it back together again.

*T*he magician takes a rope and cuts off the ends. Then he gathers the remainder of the rope and forms a loop; the loop is cut. The two pieces of rope are then reunited, magically.

A piece of rope that can be seen clearly by the audience and a scissors will be needed for this trick.

The secret:

Cut the ends of the rope. This is done for dramatic purposes. It also proves that the scissors and the rope are real. Last, it leaves an impression with the audience that the rope was cut right in front of them.

Leave the middle (the remainder) of the rope on the table. Put the freshly cut ends on the table and pick up the middle section of the rope. Place the first end between your thumb and forefinger. Take the other end and place it between the tips of your first and second fingers. Both ends must extend about four inches above your fingers. Run the fingers of the other hand down the rope and take hold of the middle of the rope.

Reach up and grab the rope on the side near the thumb, about three inches below the tip of the rope. Pinching the rope, pull it up, thus creating a new loop. Grab the new loop with your thumb. Let go of an end of the rope and show the audience that the rope is divided into two almost identical parts. Cut the rope in the loop and drop down the other end. The two parts are not identical, so you grab hold of the ends and pull them directly toward you while pulling the other end directly toward the audience. Pull the shorter end to make both sides the same length. You have created two pieces of rope, one long and one very short. The audience is not aware of this.

Now take one end and place it in the crevice of your thumb. Hold the two ends of the short rope and its hidden loop at the tips of your fingers. Hold the other end in your other hand about halfway up your palm. Use that hand to take hold of one of the short ends. Drop everything else and show you have restored the rope to its original state. If you have a table or someone standing next to you, you may drop the short rope behind them, if not, just fold everything and put it all away.

49

INDIAN ROPE TRICK

Climb a rope that rises by itself into the air.

_I_ mmensely popular at the turn of the century, this is a trick I consider a forgotten gem of magic performance since it is not performed by any modern magicians.

This illusion has been performed both outside in the open and inside on the stage.

The magician brings a small wicker basket to the center of the performing area. From within the basket a rope is withdrawn. The magician throws the rope into the air, once and then again. On the third try, the rope not only remains in the air but also continues to move up and out of the basket, rising ever higher and higher.

At some point, the rope is so high the audience can no longer see the top end of the rope. Then a young assistant climbs up the rope and continues to climb until the assistant, too, is out of sight. At this moment, the magician fires a pistol, the rope falls back to the stage, and the assistant is gone.

THE SECRET:

As you have seen in other illusions in this book, this trick has several solutions. Moreover, this particular trick is filled with controversy, too. It seems that no one ever really saw the original version of this trick. In the original version, fake holy men (actually magicians) claimed the event worked just as indicated, with no trickery. I do not know whether this assertion is true or not. However, I can say with certainty that in all my research, I have not found a single authentic viewing of this spectacle.

THE SECRET:

The illusion is based on a rope that has a hook on one end. The hook is like that found on a hitch. A thin strand of metal wire is strung across the top of the stage. The wire must be strong enough to support both the rope and the assistant. In this version, the rope is hooked to the metal strand on one of the throws. Doing this trick is easier than it sounds.

In another, more modern, version, the end of the rope is connected to a metal wire from the beginning. It is given enough slack so that it does not stifle the movement of the basket at the beginning of the illusion. The throwing of the rope is not really needed, but it does misdirect the audience.

The wire is attached to a pulley system or winch. At the right moment, the backstage assistant will turn on the pulley and lift the rope into the air. The disappearing assistant merely climbs the straightened rope and then climbs into the rafter area above the curtain lines. The act often is accompanied with smoke filling the air above the rope. This way the assistant appears to have vanished into a cloud of smoke.

Sometimes, for heightened effect, the magician will "snake charm" the rope out of the basket instead of lifting it out or throwing it up. Or the assistant could climb aboard the rope when it is only a couple of feet out of the basket. The rope then continues to climb with the assistant aboard. This technique is easier than finding someone strong enough to actually climb the rope.

The assistant does not need to vanish

at the top of the rope, especially if there is nowhere for the assistant to do so. The assistant can just climb back down. After all, the rising rope is the trick.

This is one of those illusions many have heard about but few have seen. It is in movies such as *Aladdin* or *Ali Baba and the Forty Thieves.*

Although equipment such as pulleys and winches is needed to pull this one off, it is a simple trick with a good visual effect.

When floating, beware of camera angles and lighting. It will ruin the effect when the wires are seen. Of course, everyone knows that wires are used. They simply do not want to see them. The lesson here: Be sure to hide the trick's secret when you perform. As you can see, this effect worked along the same lines. However, I would not recommend you try to float across a gap as big as the Grand Canyon.

PART FOUR

GREAT ESCAPES

50

UNDERWATER CRATE ESCAPE

How to escape from a packing case that is under water

T he magician is tied up or handcuffed, then nailed into a packing case. The packing case is lowered into the water. Minutes pass; finally, just when all seems lost and the case is about to be lifted out of the water, out of the water pops the magician, free of the constraints and the packing case.

THE SECRET:

The case has a false side that opens in; the magician has underwater breathing equipment hidden in the case, too.

The packing case is real enough. Usually it doubles for the shipping of the magician's equipment during travel days. The false panel or side, which opens in, is controlled by a hook system. Inside of the case is a mini-underwater breathing system, the same one used by short-dive swimmers. It is usually good for ten or fifteen minutes of underwater breathing.

Once the magician has been tied up, he or she crouches in the case as assistants nail it shut. By the end of the nailing process, which can take up to fifteen minutes, the magician is already out of the constraints. Once in the water, with the breathing apparatus in place, the magician will wait until the right moment to simply swim out of the case through the secret hatch. Usually after seven or eight minutes, the magician will surface.

To add to the dramatics, have a large timer with ten minutes on it. The first five minutes are in red, the rest are in black. The audience will be asked to hold its breath along with the magician. Most will give up in a minute or two. Once the five-minute mark has passed, no one will be holding his or her breath any longer. At the six-minute mark, the assistants pretend to be worried. The worry grows at the seven-minute mark, and at eight minutes they are beside themselves with worry. "Pull him up!" "Call the medics!" they will scream. However, just then the magician will surface. WOW!

51

BURNING BOX ESCAPE

Being chained inside a burning box suspended over water and surviving

*H*ere is one of my tricks that no magician has successfully copied. The magician is handcuffed with many pairs of handcuffs, ropes, locks, and chains, then nailed into a packing crate. The crate is raised off the ground and into the air by a large crane. A long wick hangs down from the crate and is lit with a torch. The entire crate had been previously covered with gasoline. The crate, with the burning wick, is swung out over the ocean, lake, bay, or pool. The trick here is for the magician to escape from the crate before the wick ignites the crate, roasting the magician.

Before the magician can escape, the crate begins to burn. At that same moment the crate seems to explode and falls into the ocean. I should also mention that this trick is best done at night. A large searchlight follows the falling crate. Has the magician died? Is this his last show? Oh, no! The searchlight moves back up to the top of the crane, and there, lo and behold, is the magician. Free, safe, and magnificent. I am getting goose bumps.

THE SECRET:

This is more than a one-secret trick. However, it is a good one.

The crate, its construction, and the handcuffs, are not important. No one is going to check them for authenticity. So don't worry that the audience will find out that the handcuffs are fake or that you have the keys. The lid of the crate is the most important part of this trick. The rope, which is used to elevate the crate off the ground, passes through a hole located in the center of the top of the crate. This same rope continues into the box and is attached to a sling-type swing. The swing will hang down halfway into the crate. The crate is big. It needs to be in order to be seen at night by a large crowd and for the trick to work well. I suggest a crate about five feet tall, three feet wide, and three feet deep.

The lid is nailed into a rail of soft pine running around the top inner lip of the crate. (Of course, the lid is not nailed onto the crate until the magician has entered the crate.)

The crate is splashed with a liquid contained in a gasoline jug. However, it is not gas. Kerosene works well and burns slowly. The wick is simply a loose cord rope, which has also been saturated with kerosene. Here is what happens:

1. The magician is tied or chained up and then placed into the crate.

2. Workers (secretly hired by the magician) gather around the box, look it over, then begin to nail it shut. While this is happening, the magician is busy freeing himself. Keys can be used, but I suggest using toy handcuffs, locks, crummy chains, and weak ropes. It does not have to be real. It just has to look good.

3. The lid is nailed onto the crate. In the meanwhile, the magician sits in the swing. At this point, the magician is swinging freely in the box, elevated off the floor of the box by the swing. If the swing does not hold now, it never will and the trick should be over. However, if the swing is holding, as it should be, then the tricky part is over. Since the workers nailed short nails into soft pine when securing the lid, the crate is not really that "together."

4. The crate is hoisted about three feet off the ground. The ignitable liquid is splashed on the wick and the crate. The magician is still swinging freely on the swing inside the box. The box has air holes, but only on the upper sides, not on the bottom or lower sides.

5. The wick is lit.

6. The crate is raised and swung out over the ocean or the pool.

7. The fire ignites the crate.

8. The crate begins to burn.

9. The magician gives the bottom of the crate a kick, and the crate slips from the short nails from the lid and drops into the water. The magician is still swinging, but now the crate is gone.

10. The spotlight follows the crate down into the water.

11. The crate floats around in the glow of the spotlight, then the spotlight moves up to reveal the magician on the swing, happily waving to the crowd.

Some footnotes:

Wireless communication between the magician and the crew is important for timing and safety. If the box does not fall on the first kick or two from the magician, the magician can reach into the air holes and pull the crate away from the lid. The short nails and the soft pine make for an easy fall from the nails in the lid.

In the past, the air holes were also used to notify the magician when the crate was actually burning, but wireless communication is a better method. The air holes make breathing more comfortable for the magician who is in the box.

Finally, children or beginners should not do this trick. Do not try it without a professional crew, setup, and safety precautions in place.

52

STRAIGHTJACKET ESCAPE

How to get out of a regulation straightjacket

*H*oudini undoubtedly made this trick most famous. Over the years, many great magicians have used this escape as a means of attracting media attention. The Amazing Randi continued to use this escape in the best Houdini fashion during the late 1960s and the early 1970s. I astonished the world in 1976 with a new twist on the escape. Rather than taking a long time to get out of the straightjacket, twisting and struggling to release myself, I escaped in a few seconds. *The Guinness Book of World Records* chose to add the speedy escape to the record books.

However, the escape is the same whether it is done quickly or slowly. Members of the audience are invited to the stage and can fully inspect the straightjacket. Most straightjackets have buckles on the back, sleeves without hand openings, and a buckle with strap on the sleeve ends. The magician is placed in the jacket and the rear buckles are fastened as tightly as possible. Then the arms are crossed in front of the magician and they, too, are fastened securely behind the magician's back. Some straightjackets also have a crotch strap that is secured, too. After all the straps and buckles are in place, the magician is able to pull free of the straightjacket in fairly short order.

THE SECRET:

While not all straightjackets are the same, I will deal with the basic hospital supply house–style jacket.

That kind of jacket comes in three sizes: small, medium, and large. Make sure you try on the jackets to ensure proper fit. Not too tight and not too loose. When the back buckles are being tightened, do not just stand there; move around as you are being fastened. As your captors pull on the straps to tighten the jacket, move back toward them as they pull. Take small breaths and keep your stomach and chest expanded as much as possible. Your expanded chest and stomach will make it more difficult for you to be tied up too tightly to move. When they are through with your back and crotch strap, they will start on your arm strap. When they cross your arms in front of you, make sure your stronger arm is on the top. Resist as they are tying you in. Do not just stand there. Keep as much resistance as you can—without letting anyone know what you are doing, of course. Once they are done, have them step off to one side and take a bow.

When you are ready to begin your escape, start by moving your top arm up to your opposite shoulder. This is done by sliding your arm up the opposite arm to the opposite shoulder. To illustrate, if your top arm is the right arm, you will move the right hand and arm up the left side of your body. Then up onto the left shoulder. Once you reach this point, you must pull this arm up over your head. Do not resist with the other arm. Remember that the strap has them hooked together. If you are pulling with both arms, you will not get too far.

Once your arms are up over your head, you can reach down toward the top buckle on your back. Through the sleeve material, your hands can grab the buckle and pull it free. Now, with the top buckle undone, you pull your arms down to your crotch strap and pull this one free, too. At this point, you can pull the entire jacket off over your head. You are out.

ANOTHER POINT:

Never used fake straightjackets. Most fake jackets have secret ways to escape. Many magicians not only like to have the jackets fully examined by the audience, but they also like to put a member of the audience into the jacket and let him or her have a go at escaping. In addition, fake jackets bought at magic shops can sell for as much as $400. The real thing, available from hospital supply houses, can be as cheap as $50. This decision is a no-brainer.

53

SUSPENDED STRAIGHTJACKET ESCAPE

Escaping from a straightjacket while suspended
upside down from a beam

*T*he magician is strapped into a regulation straightjacket. His feet are tied together, and he is hoisted up into the air. Hanging headfirst, above the ground, the magician makes his escape from the straightjacket.

THE SECRET:

This is the trick most people think about when the name Houdini is mentioned. The Amazing Randi also made a name for himself with this trick, as did many others. The trick is simple enough: the magician gets out of a straightjacket. It is the fact that the magician is dangling headfirst above the ground—or Niagara Falls, for that matter—that makes it appear so scary.

An examination of the trick will show otherwise. A straight-jacket is made of heavy canvas, leather straps, and metal buckles. When the magician is hanging upside down, gravity is pulling the jacket. In many cases, the magician has to keep the straightjacket from falling off.

Escaping from a straightjacket is not too complicated, simply a matter of pulling your arms up over your head, then wriggling out. Since gravity is pulling on the heavy jacket, you have an ally. The important factor is making certain your feet are well connected and the hoist is in good shape.

The first time I did this trick I was a sixteen-year-old student at William Lyon Mackenzie Collegiate Institute in Toronto, Canada. It was the mid-winter break celebration. The students put on plays, bands performed, and the highlight was to be me doing this upside-down straightjacket escape.

Since I was young, the budget was small. My friend John Paolucci handled the rigging while another pal, Lloyd Segal, handled curtains and lights.

A local television station was there to catch all the action. The lights dimmed, flash and smoke pots went off, and the curtain was to open, revealing me suspended upside down in a straightjacket twenty feet above the stage. I remember seeing the curtains opening, and I can still recall my body slowly beginning to spin. Then came the crash.

It seems that the curtain wire and the hoist wires got crossed. Before I knew it, the hoist broke loose and I was headed down to the stage like a scud missile. I hit the ladder, broke a chair, and nearly broke my neck. After being rushed to the hospital for stitches, I got home in time to watch it all unfold on the evening news.

Why am I telling you all of this? Simply because I do not want what happened to me to happen to anyone else.

If you want to do a trick like this, or any other dangerous trick, get someone to help you through it. Do not try to do it on your own. Be careful. That way you, too, can live to tell the story.

54

GREAT HANDCUFF ESCAPE

The magician escapes from a
pair of regulation handcuffs.

When I first began to do magic and escapes, I once had a chance to perform this trick on a television show live from an exhibition ground. It was at a moment's notice, and I did not want to miss the opportunity. All I had was a pair of handcuffs, but the trick went over big.

The trick goes like this: You invite three or four people up onstage. Each gets a chance to examine the handcuffs, check out how the key can lock and unlock the cuffs, and examine a plain brown paper bag.

Your sleeves are rolled up and your arms and hands are examined. Once the audience members are satisfied, you are handcuffed and the paper bag is slipped over your hands. Before they can count to three, you rip off the paper bag, revealing that you have gotten out of the cuffs and are free.

THE SECRET:

The cuffs are real and can belong to anyone. In the case mentioned here, I actually borrowed a pair of handcuffs from one of Toronto's finest. I invited three people onstage; the police officer whose cuffs were used and two other people from the audience. Each had to check out the cuffs and the key. The cuffs were locked onto my wrists. I shook hands with the police officer and the other two, then had my hands covered with the bag.

How did I get out? Elementary, my dear Watson. The last person to shake my hand was a friend of mine; he slipped me the key as he shook my hand. Then my hands were covered with the bag.

When I asked the audience to count to three, I was already out of the cuffs. At the count of three I tore the bag off my hands and revealed the cuffs in my left hand.

This time, the first hand I shook was that of my friend, secretly giving him back the key. Then I shook the hands of the other two and returned the cuffs to the officer. He collected the key from my accomplice and no one was any wiser.

55

HAND STOCK ESCAPE

Escape from a nineteenth-century torture device

*T*his is an easy trick to build, and is a good trick for magic newbies.

The magician tells the audience how witches were locked into stocks in nineteenth-century Salem. He allows the stocks to be examined, then gets them locked onto his wrists. Behind a small curtain, the magician is still able to move objects, ring bells, and throw balls. Yet each time the curtain is moved away, the magician is still locked securely in place.

THE SECRET:

The stock is made up of two pieces. Each is a block of wood twelve inches long and four inches high and one inch thick. Two half circles have been cut out of each block. When the two stocks are placed together, the two half circles form openings large enough to hold the wrists of the magician, yet tight enough that his hands cannot be slipped through them.

The secret of this trick is the openings themselves. When holes A and B are formed, they make a handcufflike stock that will hold the magician's wrists in place. Hole A has been drilled slightly off center high and hole B is low and a little off center.

When you rotate the top stock and place the two pieces back together, the openings appear.

Now opening A is smaller and tighter and opening B is large enough for your hand to easily slip in and out. The stocks are held in place with two padlocks (the padlocks are located along the sides).

Behind the curtain, slip your hand out of the larger opening and move the objects, then slip it back in when the curtain is removed. For the finale, slip one hand out, put your hands behind your back, and slip your hand back in. When the curtain is removed this time, turn around and show that you are sill trapped in the stocks. Have the padlocks removed and take a bow.

PART FIVE

MYSTERIOUS MAYHEM

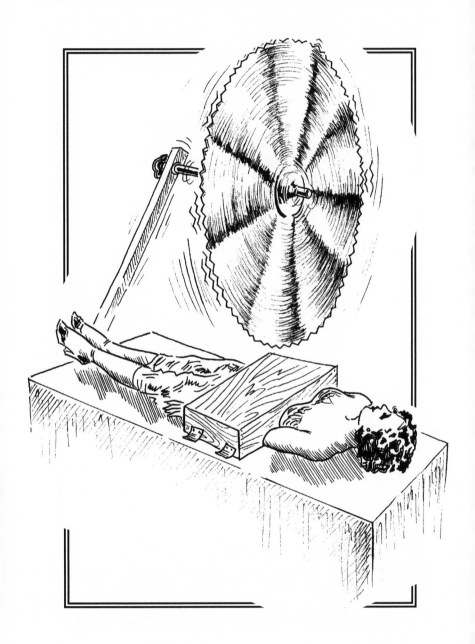

56

SAWING A PERSON IN TWO

How to saw someone in two in full view

A spectator lies on a flat board. A brace is affixed over the person's stomach and is attached to the board on which she or he is lying. An electric jigsaw is brought out, and the magician proceeds to saw across the spectator's midsection as the saw is run through the brace.

The brace is removed and the spectator walks away in one piece.

THE SECRET:

The blade in the jigsaw is a fake. The blade is specially made to dislodge from the saw when it enters the far side of the brace. Another blade is waiting at the end of the brace. The second blade connects to the jigsaw as you exit the body brace. This jigsaw is available at most of the larger magic shops, along with the board and the brace.

The jigsaw is an everyday object and should make a lot of noise. This is good because many people should be familiar with the sound of the saw. Too much magic is done with objects that

are strange or rare. Even such items as swords, daggers, and guil-
lotines are not commonly found anywhere except in museums.
These types of items might make the audience dubious right from
the start.

Some magicians go to great lengths to look cool and modern.
Then they bring out-of-date props into their ultramodern shows. If
you want to succeed as a magician, stay away from the silly an-
tique tricks that dominate magic stores and catalogs. Look at
everyday objects and ask yourself, "What can I do with them?"
Then go out and make some magic.

57

SAWING IN HALF—SIMPLE

How to separate the upper body from the lower

A girl is placed into a thin version of the "sawing a person in two" illusion. Side doors are opened to reveal the girl's arms and legs; her feet and head protrude from the box. The doors are closed, large blades are inserted into the midsection of the box, and the box is separated, distancing the girl's lower part from her upper part. The doors are reopened to show her arms and legs, and her feet move when tickled. She is put back together and steps out unharmed.

THE SECRET:

The box that holds the girl's upper part is large enough for the entire girl. Just as I dislike using animals, it pains me to see that female assistants must do such contortions in order to do a trick. This box is very thin, but the girl has just enough space to curl up her body in the small box.

Her legs never actually go into the lower half of the box, except to push the false feet out of the far end. Then she curls up into the upper half of the box. The legs, which are shown, are fake, just like the feet. The arm is real enough. Her body cannot be seen because of the following:

1. The darkness of the interior of the box
2. The dark dress she is wearing
3. Her arm blocks the view lines into the box.

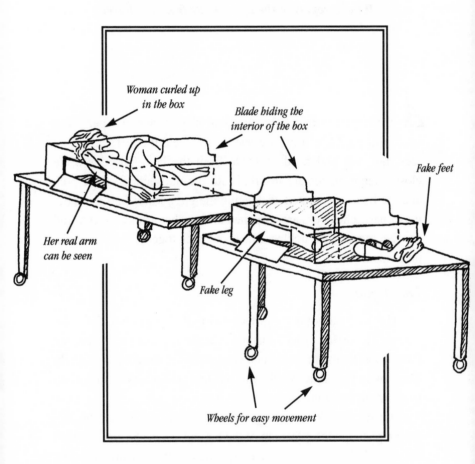

Woman curled up in the box

Blade hiding the interior of the box

Fake feet

Her real arm can be seen

Fake leg

Wheels for easy movement

The blades actually block off the ends of the boxes by filling the opening created when the boxes are separated. The feet can move by way of a string or rope, which is attached to a spring system. Pulling the string moves the feet back and forth.

The halves of the box are then rejoined, the blades are removed, the feet are withdrawn, the top is opened, and out pops the girl. Not many angles to worry about with this trick. The real trick is getting the audience to believe that the feet and legs are real.

This is a standard magic trick. Whether it can still be used in magic today is questionable. There was a time when people fainted at the sight of a woman being sawed in half. Today, most people know that no harm comes to the woman in the box, but audiences might still enjoy the mystery.

58

REMOVING THE MIDDLE

Remove a woman's midsection painlessly

*T*his illusion is popular with many of today's most successful magicians. It is kin to Sawing in Half.

This illusion has been used with lasers and sometimes the magician, rather than the assistant, is the subject. It is an interesting puzzle no matter how it is done. A box similar to one used in the Sawing in Half—Simple trick is center stage. A person lies down in the box with head and feet protruding from opposite ends.

Side panels are opened to reveal the body profile of the occupant in the box. After large blades are inserted just below the neck and just above the ankles, the middle section is removed from the table. Then, to the delight of the magician, the feet and the head sections slowly begin to move toward each other until the feet appear to be growing out of the neck of the subject. All the while the feet move and the head can talk and smile. At the end, the feet and head return to their original positions, the middle section is returned, and the subject steps out of the box, unaffected by wear.

THE SECRET:

As with most magic tables, this table is not as thin as it appears. The subject enters the box and uses his or her own feet to push out a pair of false feet constructed into the other end of the box. When the side panels are opened, the subject's arm is the only body part that really belongs to the person in the box. What appears to be the torso, legs, and feet are only make-believe. The real body of the subject is submerged into the table cavity, hidden from the audience.

Once the side doors are shut, the subject completely submerges into the hollow of the special table. As the head and feet sections seemingly move together, the subject is actually sliding along a conveyer belt toward the fake mechanical feet. The submerged subject easily controls the feet.

Once all the sections are put back together, the assistant moves the fake feet back into the box. The side panels cover this movement. Then the assistant steps out of the box to join the magician and take their bows.

This is a great, angle-proof trick, similar to Mismatch Woman, but has a more modern look and feel to it. Most of the time, the subject appears to be uncomfortable during the "shortening" effect.

Do not let the simplicity of this trick throw you. It can really fool the audience.

59

SAWING IN TWO—ROPE VERSION

The magician is able to create the illusion that
he has cut the woman in two with a rope.

T he magician asks a woman from the audience to join him on-stage. A rope is placed around her and tied with a knot. The magician takes the ends of the rope and makes the rope pass through the woman, as if she has been cut in two.

THE PROPS:

Two pieces of rope, each sixty inches in length, and a rubber band.

THE SECRET:

To prepare the trick, fold both ropes in two, creating loops right in the middle. Secure the two loops together with the rubber band. Hold the secured loops in the palm of your hand so they are hidden from view. Place the secured loops behind the volunteer's back and bring the ends forward around her body. Tie any two ends in a simple knot, not too tightly. Hold the ends in one hand and pull them to the side. At the same time, pull forward. The rubber band will break. When the ropes come free, show them to the volunteer so she can see that they are solid ropes.

60

CUTTING INTO FOURTHS

Dividing your victim into four quarters

This is a "big" stage trick. The magician shows a rectangular box (the box is about the size of a coffin) resting on a small-wheeled platform. The box is actually made up of four separate boxes, sitting side by side. Doors on all four boxes are opened and the magician's assistant lies down inside the boxes. The doors are closed. The only things you see are the hands of the assistant, which are sticking up through the top of the number two box.

The magician proceeds to slice through the box with giant blades (cards, saws, etc). The blades seem to pass right through the assistant and down through the table. The assistant has been cut into fourths. Nevertheless, her hands can still be seen!

THE SECRET:

You need four boxes, each with a front door facing the audience and a top, which also opens. Each box is two feet tall, two feet wide, and one and a half feet long. End to end, the four boxes measure six feet in length (one and a half times four). The four boxes are mounted on a wheeled platform. There is a slight space between each box, about half an inch, just large enough to allow you to insert your item of penetration (the blade). The platform has a spandex inner surface. Once your assistant enters the boxes, and the doors have been closed, the assistant slides down into the well of the spandex platform. The hands continue to be seen due to the twenty-four-inch height of the boxes. Although the assistant is in the spandex well, his or her arms should be long enough to reach up through the openings for the hands.

I think I saw magician Mark Wilson doing this trick back in the early seventies. I have not seen anyone do it since.

61

THE INVISIBLE BECOMES VISIBLE

How to make someone appear out of nowhere.

Normally this trick is used to introduce the magician at the start of the magic show. An assistant is resting on a small table located in the center of the stage. Two stagehands come out, rotate the table, and then lift a curtain up off the table and over the assistant, now standing on the table. Just as quickly as the small curtain has been raised to conceal the assistant, it is lowered again. The assistant has now been joined by the magician, and the two of them are standing in a fashion pose. The magician jumps down off the table and the show begins.

It is a common trick for magicians to make someone appear from what is plain sight. In this case, a small table is resting in the center of the stage. The audience can clearly see above and below the table. Sitting on the table is the magician or the magician's assistant. The table is rotated, and then the person on the table stands up. A curtain, just large enough to cover the person on the table, is then lifted from the table and placed over the person standing on the table. Just as quickly as the curtain has gone up around the person standing on the table, it is taken away. Okay, I have said it twice; now you have the picture.

THE SECRET:

In a word, spandex, the strong, flexible material that has become a great friend to the magician. In this case, the table upon which this trick is done is specially made and spandex plays a big part in its construction.

The table is hollow, with an opening just large enough for the magician to be lying in it. The table dimensions are as follows: five feet long, three feet wide, and legs twenty-six to thirty inches high, with wheels or casters on the bottom. A raised section appears ten inches in from the edges of the table. The raised section appears as a stepped-up area in the center of the table. Below this area, extending under the table, is the spandex basin. The center step is three to five inches high. This height, added to the spandex depth of three to five inches, and coupled with the thickness of the table itself, two to three inches, totals almost thirteen inches of hiding space, space in which the magician or assistant is lying, hidden from the audience. Only half of the step area has actual step space. The back portion of the step has no top. When standing on the table, the magician can see the face and upper portion of the person lying below. No moving parts are needed on this table. When the curtain goes up around the person standing on the table, the other person, secreted away in the step, will slip up out of the spandex cocoon and join the first person up on the step.

THE PRESENTATION:

The table is wheeled out onto the stage and is spun around for effect. A hoop draped with a curtain (such as the one used in the Metamorphosis trick on page 201) is placed onto the table. The circumference of the hoop is just greater than the step on top of the table. The magician gets up on the table and stands on the step (or there has been someone on the table from the beginning).

The hoop-draped curtain is brought up around the magician only as high as his chest. The magician speaks a few choice words, giving the person hidden in the table a chance to climb out and onto the step. Although still in a crouching position, hidden from view behind the hoop-draped curtain, the second person gets ready to appear.

In a flash, the magician lifts the curtain over his or her head. This is the moment when the once-hidden person stands up to join the magician. Just as fast as the curtain has gone up, it is dropped, exposing the magician and the newly appeared second individual. The last movement of the curtain (up and down) should be done very quickly for the most dramatic effect.

62

GUILLOTINE

Cutting off the head of a spectator—who survives

*P*lace a large, awesome French guillotine in the center of the stage. A hapless audience member has been chosen to put her or his neck into the stock. Suspended several feet above is a shiny metal blade. Once the audience member is locked into the head-stock, the giant blade is released and it comes crashing down. The audience sees the blade come down, then seemingly pass right through the audience member's neck until it reaches the bottom of the guillotine. The victim, of course, has survived with her or his neck intact.

THE SECRET:

Two blades, both fakes. Whether you call this the French, Super, or Super-Duper Guillotine, it produces the same sort of effect. The top blade only goes as far as the inside of the top neck stock. It can go no farther and cannot touch the neck of the victim because a stopper is located in the top neck stop. The stopper is a shelflike piece of wood that protects the neck. The first blade releases the second blade from underneath the neck of the victim, where it was concealed in the lower portion of the stock.

On occasion magicians will cut a head of lettuce in half first. How do they do that? The lettuce has been precut and is held together with a toothpick. The magician is holding the head of lettuce in the stock hole. The blade crashes down, the lettuce is bumped against the stock (by the magician) at the moment of intended impact, and the lettuce breaks in two. The blade travels so quickly, no one notices that it never went through the stock hole opening. While assistants put everything back in place, the magician picks the audience member. The assistants will block the audience's view of the blade replacements and do so quickly. That way no one notices the two blades. It is all smoke and mirrors.

This is a real dead-end trick. It is anticlimactic. Once the blade fails to cut off the head, there is nothing more to do. Some suggest that you close your show at this point. You know, drop the blade and then close the stage curtain. No one knows if it has worked or not. Might be a bit gruesome, but one magician actually had a scream sound track play when the blade hit, then quickly closed the curtain.

A newer version of this effect uses what is called a breakaway just below the spectator's neck. A breakaway is a pressure release opening. When the top blade strikes, the breakaway opens, allowing the spectator to drop down out of the stock and below the stock area. Then the breakaway, using springs, returns to its proper position. If you had a basket in front of the guillotine, it might appear that the head had been cut off and fell into the basket.

How about adding spurting blood and fake heads? It's all been done. However, no matter what you do with this trick, it should end the act.

63

SWORD THROUGH THE NECK

***A sword is thrust through an individual's neck
without cutting him***

A metal sword is handed to a member of the audience; meanwhile, a metal collar is locked around the neck of another audience member. Once the first audience member has verified the sword's authenticity, it is returned to the magician. The sword is thrust through a slot in the metal collar and straight out the other side, appearing to have gone through the neck of the surprised spectator.

THE SECRET:

There are two sword blades. When the first "sword" is handed for examination to an individual in the audience, it is solid enough. This is because attached to the sword's handle is a solid metal sword shaft. When the magician has the sword handed back to him, he inserts it into its sheath. While the sword is being inserted into the sheath, the magician presses a secret button on the sword handle, releasing the solid metal sword shaft. Waiting inside the sheath is another shaft; this one is made of flexible aluminum. The handle is connected to this second shaft under the cover of the sheath.

Then the magician attaches the collar around the neck of the spectator. The collar has two channels, only one of which goes through the center. When the sword is plunged into the collar, it actually goes into the second channel, which, in its gimmicked way, runs the flexible sword blade around the neck and out the other side of the collar.

This is the same trick as the well-known standard Sword Through the Neck; the only difference is the *fake* blade. I have seen both, and switching the blades on the two-blade version is hard to do. In addition, for the amount of impact one gets, I would suggest that beginners stay with the standard version.

The standard Sword Through the Neck version uses a neck collar that has two openings in which the sword can enter. One opening is normal enough, meaning that the sword will go in one side, pierce whatever is in the collar, and then come out the other end of the collar. The other opening is a channel that runs through the interior of the collar. The sword blade is flexible spring steel. It will enter the channel and safely move around the inside of the collar, then out the other end, never having been exposed to the person's neck—or anything else that might be in the collar, such as a balloon.

The most fun to have with this trick is to choose a squeamish-looking person from the audience as the potential victim. Blow up a balloon and have the "victim" hold the balloon in the collar. Thrust the sword through the balloon. Of course, you will use the normal channel and the balloon will burst. The spectator will jump and everyone will laugh. Then get the spectator into the collar and do some magic.

64

HEAD DAGGER—DELUXE

**Daggers are thrust into a spectator's head,
but the spectator survives.**

A spectator is seated onstage, and a large box is placed on a pedestal in front of the spectator. The spectator places his or her head into the rear of the box; the audience can see the spectator through the front opening of the box. A rear door is closed behind the spectator's head, and then front doors are moved into place, concealing the spectator in the box. Fifteen daggers are thrust into the box from all directions. The front doors are opened and, to the surprise of the audience, the spectator's head is gone, but all the daggers can be clearly seen. The doors are replaced, the daggers are removed, and the victim's head reappears.

THE SECRET:

Mirrors! On the inside of the box are two mirrors hinged to the sides of the box. Once the front doors are in place, the magician releases two controls that move the mirrors into a forty-five-degree angle toward the front of the box. The center of the mirrors (where they meet) is hidden by the first dagger, which is thrust downward into the box from the top. The rest of the daggers merely slide up against the mirror or harmlessly behind the spectator's head.

When the front doors are opened, the audience actually sees the reflection of the interior box sides via the mirrors. The box appears to be filled with daggers from every direction, but this is actually the mirrors reflecting the daggers.

PART SIX

MIND READING

65

BOOK READING

The magician is able to read the words from a book that is not in the magician's possession.

*T*he magician displays two books. He asks that one of them be chosen by a spectator. The magician then asks that the spectator randomly choose a page from the book. The books are exchanged, and the spectator now turns to the same page of the second book as he or she chose from the first book. The magician then tells the spectator what is on this page.

THE SECRET:

To prepare yourself for this trick you will need any two randomly chosen books. Take one of the books as though to check it, and look through it. Randomly stop at a page and memorize the page number and a few words from the top and some from farther down the page. Ask a volunteer to choose one of the books. If the volunteer chooses the book you looked at, put it down on the table in plain view and ask him or her to go through the other book. This is the same as forcing a card: you offer two books but you control which book will be chosen. If the volunteer chooses the other book, ask him or her to go through it and stop at any one of the pages.

As the volunteer makes the page choice, you take the book away. Do not let the volunteer see the page he or she has chosen, merely allow him or her to simply open the book to a page. Tell the volunteer to take the other book and turn to the page he or she chose in the first book. This is the page you chose earlier, but you are letting the volunteer think it is the page that he or she just chose. Once the volunteer has opened the book to the right page, you make a great act out of reading his or her mind.

66

MIND READING—
BLACK MAGIC STYLE

Find chosen items without anyone's help

*A*fter talking about psychics and black magic, the magician offers a demonstration in mind reading. The magician then asks someone from the audience to assist by touching any object or objects in the room while the magician is out of the room. The magician leaves the room, objects are touched, then the magician returns. The magician now asks for a second member of the audience to participate by coming forward and randomly pointing at objects around the room. Not a single word is spoken as the magician concentrates and carefully watches the spectator point.

Suddenly the magician says, "Stop!" To everyone's amazement, the object stopped at is one of the chosen objects.

THE SECRET:

Not one single word is spoken between you and the second spectator, but it is this second spectator who signals to you which objects were chosen. This person, also known as a confederate, can have his or her back you to while pointing, so there is no eye contact. You can also stress the fact that there is complete silence throughout. But how *do* you get the signal? The answer is black magic, of course!

This explanation is much nearer to the truth than you would expect. You receive the signal while your confederate points at random objects around the room. The signal is as follows: Just before your confederate points to the chosen object he must point to a black object. This, of course, is easy for you to pick up. The trick can be repeated, but the more astute members of your audience will soon catch on that a signal is being used, so try to vary the amount and the order of objects being pointed to!

67

MESSAGE READING

**The magician reveals a secret message
without touching the sealed envelope containing it.**

*T*he magician hands a stack of envelopes, a pencil, and a piece of paper to a member of the audience, directing this person to write a few words to a loved one. Once the audience member is done, have him or her return the pencil and the envelopes. Have him or her fold the secret message, then hand him or her one envelope and have the audience member seal the message in the envelope.

After a few moments, the magician reveals the contents of the message without ever having touched the sealed envelope that holds the message.

THE SECRET:

The top and bottom envelopes each contain a piece of carbon paper. Logically, when you hand out the pencil, the envelopes, and the slip of paper, the audience member will use the envelopes as the writing surface when writing the note. Have the envelopes bundled together with an elastic to keep everything together.

When the envelope bundle and the pencil are returned to you, remove an envelope from the center of the pack to give back to the audience member. While the spectator is busy sealing the message into the envelope, peek into the envelope that was used as the writing surface. The secret message will have been copied with carbon into the envelope. Memorize it and perform your miracle.

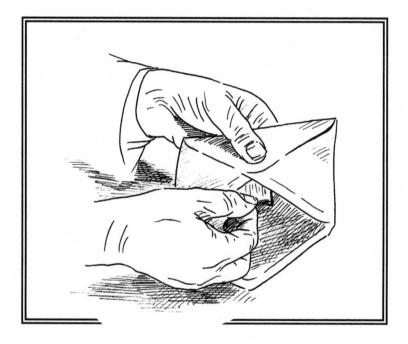

68

DICE PREDICTION

A pair of dice is shaken up, yet the magician knows what number will be on each die.

A small pair of dice is shown and rolled freely on the table. The magician then opens a box of matches and drops the dice into the box. The box is shaken, then placed on the table. The magician announces which numbers are represented on each die, and when the box is opened, the magician is correct.

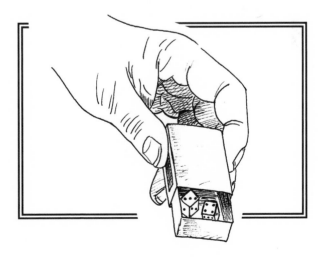

THE SECRET:

You need a regular matchbox and four dice. Glue two of the dice to the bottom of the matchbox drawer toward one side of the box. During the performance of this trick, slide the box open halfway and insert the dice. Shake the box, or have someone shake it for you. When you reopen the box, tilt it toward the end where the dice have NOT been glued. Slide the box open with the glued dice showing.

Since you know the numbers on the dice you glued into the drawer, your prediction will always be correct.

69

CARD PREDICTION

The magician predicts which index card out of three will be chosen.

*T*hree index cards are on the table. Each has a message written on it. Ask someone from the audience to mentally choose a card. Once this is done, tell the person that you have predicted the future. His or her choice was previously written down. To prove it, have the spectator announce the card chosen. The magician then reveals the prediction—and voilà, the magician is correct!

THE SECRET:

Prepare three index cards by writing the following on them:

1. $7,000,000
2. WORLD PEACE
3. IMMORTALITY

On the back of an envelope you have written "I KNEW YOU WOULD CHOOSE WORLD PEACE." On a small piece of paper, you have written "I KNEW YOU WOULD CHOOSE IMMOR-TALITY." And on the back of the $7,000,000 card you have written "I KNEW YOU WOULD CHOOSE THIS CARD." There is nothing written on the back of the other two cards.

Place the three cards on the table faceup. The envelope must contain the small piece of paper and be placed on the table so that the audience member cannot see that there is any writing on the envelope's back. Now have the volunteer choose one of the index cards. Depending upon which index card was chosen, you will either turn over the envelope, open the envelope and reveal the note, or turn the index cards over. Whichever way you go, you have the prediction.

70

NUMBER PREDICTIONS

The magician will predict the three numbers written out by three volunteers.

*T*hree volunteers each choose a number between one and one hundred. When the three numbers are added together, they equal a number that the magician had written earlier and sealed in an envelope.

THE PROPS:

A small pad of writing paper, an envelope containing the prediction, and a pen.

THE SECRET:

Prepare the pad of paper so that it looks the same from both sides. (Some pads have cardboard on one side; preparing the pad would mean removing this cardboard.) In this manner, you have a plain pad of paper. On one side of the pad, write three numbers that when added total the amount written on your prediction. Turn the pad over and place it facedown on the table. Ask three volunteers to each write one number on the pad while it is on the table (don't let them pick it up). Hand them a pen and show them where you want the numbers written. After the three people have finished writing the numbers, you take the pen back and thank them for their help.

Ask one of the volunteers to hold the envelope. Pick up the pad, turn it over, and walk over to a fourth volunteer. Remove the top page and hand it to this person. This top page was the previous bottom page, the page on which the magician wrote three numbers previously. Ask the fourth person to total up the three numbers on the paper. When he or she has the numbers totaled up, ask the first volunteer to open the envelope and show everyone your prediction.

This trick works because the first three people each wrote a number. The sheet of paper you gave to the fourth person was not the page the three volunteers wrote their numbers on. It was the page the magician prepared previously. The fourth volunteer did not see the numbers written by the others and will not suspect that there has been a switch.

71

ESP AND SOCIAL SECURITY NUMBERS

Read the thoughts of people in the audience.

*M*agicians always fool the audience when they seem to be able to read thoughts of people in the crowd. Reciting someone's Social Security number continues to be one of the most popular tricks.

The magician takes to the stage and, with a pad of paper in hand, begins to write down thoughts that are supposedly being transmitted to him from members of the audience. The magician calls out a person's name. That person stands and the magician talks about personal things surrounding this spectator, facts that only a mind reader could know. The magician continues to surprise members of the audience while seemingly reading the minds of many in the crowd.

The secret:

This trick is simple to describe and even easier to perform. The real trick here is to not bore the audience too much as you read their thoughts. The truth is simple: The magician does not know anyone in the audience, so there are no plants among them. He could not possibly know that much about each person. Even if the magician used an expensive listening device such as a Whisper 2000, not enough information could be gathered to make this trick hold up.

So how does the magician do it? Simple. The audience volunteers the information. As the audience files in, whether the show is being performed in a nightclub or a theater, selected people are handed a clipboard and pen. They are instructed to write down anything they wish to have "read" by the magician. They are told that the magician will never see the sheet that they have written, nor will anyone else. Once they have written their innermost thoughts, they are told to seal the paper inside an envelope and keep it in their possession.

Instructions on the clipboard usually give the audience member ideas for items to write down, such as Social Security numbers, names of children and parents, birth dates, anniversary dates, etc. Writing down this information takes place long before the magician takes to the stage. Not all the members of the audience will be asked to be part of the experiment. That would just take too much time. After the staff recovers the clipboards and pens, there will be no further mention of the writings. In other words, when the magician takes to the stage, he or she will not thank those people for writing their thoughts down on paper.

At some point during the show, the magician will simply go into a mind reading routine. Those people who were given the clipboards were also told that during this segment of the show they should stand when the magician mentioned something they had written down. This way they will become part of the show. People like to be part of the show.

THE SECRET:

The clipboards have a special function. Whatever is written on the clipboard paper is carbonized onto a paper in a secret compartment inside the clipboard. When the clipboards are collected, they go to the magician, who makes notes of several messages written down by audience members. The notes are written on the same pad the magician will take out into the act.

When the magician is supposedly receiving messages telepathically, he or she is actually just reading the messages written down by members of the audience. As simple a trick as this is, the impact on an audience is overwhelming. When done on a television studio audience, it is even more amazing to the home viewers, who have no idea that the same members of the studio audience who are having their minds read actually wrote down their messages earlier. The viewers at home just think the magician is reading minds, and the people in the audience are so stunned that they automatically stand up when they hear the magician read their thoughts.

Most people will write down a Social Security number because they think it is more difficult to read than their name. Others will try to fool the magician by writing incorrect information about themselves. The magician, who sees what is written before every performance, always wins the game.

About 10 percent of the audience will get clipboards, but there will only be time to read the thoughts of half of them. Why not read them all? The spectators were not concentrating hard enough on what they had written, the magician can tell them. In reality, time constraints keep the magician from reading all the thoughts, but the magician will have asked all in the audience to think of things and will thank the entire audience for the extrasensory perception test. The magician will not say, "Those of you who wrote something down on a clipboard are to concentrate on those thoughts."

Why do the members of the audience write down their thoughts? If anyone asks this question, an assistant or the magician should say that the clipboard was supposed to make it easier for people to concentrate on the messages they were sending to the magician.

Why did the audience members keep their messages? A souvenir of the show, of course.

A TIP:

The astute magician will make this trick only a part of the show and not the entire show.

72

FIND THE PAYCHECK

Another of the great mind reading tricks is the paycheck game of hide-and-seek.

*T*he audience is invited to hide the paycheck of the magician. A member of the audience can hide the money anywhere he or she chooses. If the magician cannot find the check, the money is forfeited or given to charity. Often the magician will leave the stage or the building. It is just as effective for the magician to be blindfolded onstage, facing the back of the stage, and surrounded by a group of spectators from the audience.

Meanwhile, someone has an envelope that has been handed to him or her by the manager of the nightclub. Inside the envelope is the magician's nightly paycheck. The envelope can be hidden anywhere in the auditorium. It can go under a seat, in the purse of a spectator, or up in the air ducts.

There is no limit to possible hiding places. But wherever it is hidden, the magician is able to find the paycheck and fool the audience every time.

THE SECRET:

Again, many techniques are used to pull off this miracle. Often a magician will have several methods in place during each show. This way it becomes a safer trick because there is less chance that the trick will fail.

Once the audience is convinced that the check is hidden well, the stage committee removes the blindfold from the magician. The person who hid the check will then join the magician onstage while the members of the committee are thanked and sent back to their seats.

The remaining spectator now walks along with the magician in a challenging game similar to Hot and Cold, only the magician does not ask how close he is.

First method: A confederate has been placed in the audience before the show (a confederate is a person who works with the magician but appears to be a member of the audience). Because the entire audience knows where the money has been hidden, it is a simple matter for the confederate to let the magician know if he is close or not. While the magician moves about the theater, the accomplice uses a variety of signals to let the magician know where to go, until the magician is finally able to track down the envelope.

Second method: Either the person who hid the money or the one who is showing the magician around is the accomplice. It then becomes a simple task to lead the magician around just long enough to build up suspense for the trick. In this instance, the magician might even be blindfolded, holding the arm of the accomplice while moving about the room.

In this method, the magician can state that there is no one among the spectators who is an accomplice to this trick, even offering a reward if anyone in the audience is proven to be an accomplice. Of course, the magician can make this statement truthfully at the time when the accomplice is onstage and is not present among the audience.

Third method: The high-tech method is becoming very popular with today's magicians. Using a listening device such as a Whisper 2000, a helper backstage can listen to where the envelope is being hidden. Alternatively, using a telephoto lens, again from backstage, a helper can watch the process of hiding the envelope. Through the use of a wireless transmitter and a receiver worn by the magician, the information can be transmitted quickly and inconspicuously.

Method three can also be used when a magician comes onstage and is able to tell various people in the audience such information as their names. Other personal information can be picked up with such listening devices and used during the show. It is surprising to learn what people reveal about themselves before a show starts.

Fourth method: A trick known as Muscle Reading. The magician will hold the arm of the person who hid the envelope, who is *not* an accomplice. As he walks, the magician feels for involuntary contractions of muscles as they close in on the envelope. Although this way is the toughest, the method does have an uncanny effect. Most people will find it impossible to stay calm while the search is taking place.

A TIP:

Using more than one technique during a show will more than likely serve the purpose for the magician. It will help ensure the magician's success and leave less chance for error. This illusion obviously takes a great deal of time. You first must describe what you are going to do and why. Then you must get the committee up onstage with you. The act of hiding the check cannot be timed, because it is left up to the audience. Finding the check also takes time. I have seen this trick go on for forty minutes. If your entire show is this one trick, you might not have many bookings. If you use it as the finale, which is where this trick is best placed, you must make sure you leave yourself enough time. How will you know how much time is enough? It will take some trial and error.

PART SEVEN

MAGICAL ILLUSIONS

73

Mini Ashra

How to make a doll float and vanish

*L*evitation with dolls! Good for close-up, television, or small stage. Similar to the full stage version of the famous Ashra trick, this version is considered "cute." You be the judge.

A small doll, similar to a Barbie doll, is placed on a little bed. A cloth covers her. The cloth mystically begins to float up to a foot or more above the bed. Barbie is also obviously floating, since her form can be seen under the cloth. For the big effect, pass a hoop over the cloth. The finale is whisking the cloth off the Barbie and—voilà—she has vanished. Okay, hold on to your hats, here is the secret.

The secret:

All you need is a Barbie doll, a faked cloth, and a special bed. Here are the details. The doll is plain—it doesn't even have to be a Barbie; any doll the same size will work. You can even borrow one from your children. The bed is special. The top of the bed has two parts. A flap runs lengthwise along the bed. Place the doll on the side closest to the magician. As you bring the cloth up over the doll, you flip the front half of the flap over the doll, forcing her to sink into the recess of the bed and out of sight. Inside the cloth, a form creates a doll-like bulge. Connected to the bulge is a handle.

The bulge and the handle are sewn inside the cloth and are hidden from the audience. Once the cloth has covered the doll, grab the handle and raise the cloth up off the table.

With your free hand (the one not holding the handle), pick up a hoop, pass it over the cloth, and down onto your hand. For the finale, fling or whisk the cloth up into the air. The "doll" is gone and the trick is complete. Toss the cloth into a heap onto the table and take your bows.

74

SUCKER TEAR

Teach your audience a trick and then trick them with it.

*T*he magician teaches the audience how to do a Torn and Restored napkin, tissue, or paper towel trick. The performer takes two napkins, tears one up, and shows the audience how to use the other napkin to restore the first one. But in the end, the magician still manages to fool the audience.

THE SECRET:

Before you do this trick, secretly have a napkin rolled up and finger palmed in your right hand (a finger palm is simply holding something—in this case, a napkin—hidden in the space between your thumb and your index finger). Come up onstage holding two napkins, one in each hand, and explain to the audience that you will teach them how this trick is done the way Penn and Teller do it. Tell them to take two napkins and roll up one in their left hand, then finger palm it, which you will also do. Remember that you have another one finger palmed in your right hand.

Tell them that this is how they are to come out onstage, not telling their audience that there is a napkin in their left hand. Then you explain that they are to tear up the other one into strips and roll the strips into a ball, which you do also. However, while you roll up the strips, you switch the palmed napkin in your right hand with the torn one, thus the audience thinks that you still have the torn one. The switch takes some practice; you must execute it as you roll up the napkin you have been showing the audience. You roll it into the palm of your right hand, roll the finger palmed napkin out into your palm, and make the exchange. This is why this trick is called a sucker tear; you are suckering the crowd into believing you are doing one thing when you are really doing another.

Then you say that you will take the "torn" napkin and place it in your left hand, along with the other palmed one. While you explain the trick, you are actually showing them the moves in a "do as I do" mode. Do not let the audience see the torn napkin that is still in your right hand.

Explain that now the magician must say something to distract the audience. Remember that the magician is teaching the audience a trick and they are following along with him. The magician explains that he must make the audience look away from his left hand. In the audience, each person has two napkins in his or her left hand. The magician also has two napkins in this hand. He also has a napkin hidden in his right hand; the audience does not. This is done, so you say, so that the two napkins can be switched within the left hand, the "torn" one with the whole one.

Reach into your left pocket and pull it inside out in order to show it is empty. However, before you pull out your pocket, secretly drop the torn hidden napkin through a previously prepared small hole in the pocket. Then pinch the hole closed and pull out the pocket and show it is empty. You have cleverly disposed of the third napkin, which had been hidden in your right hand. Point out to the audience that when you pulled out your pocket, you switched the two napkins in your left hand. They, too, should switch the napkins in their left hands. Then push your pocket back in.

Tell the audience that by taking the first napkin and unfolding it, it seems as if you restored the torn napkin. They have just learned a trick that they can show to their friends. Now for the sucker part. Tell the audience that even the second napkin in the left hand can be restored by simply blowing on your hand. With that you and the audience each blow on the left hand and unfold the second napkin. Yours is restored, while the audience's are still torn. You have fooled your audience.

75

VANISHING BOWL OF WATER

A bowl filled with water vanishes in midair.

*T*he magician's assistant holds a tray that contains a bowl and a pitcher of water (or milk, colored water, or beer). The magician takes the pitcher and pours the liquid into the bowl. The magician covers the bowl with a cloth and lifts the bowl off the tray. He throws the cloth up into the air and the bowl and liquid have vanished.

THE SECRET:

The bowl is attached to the tray. Attach a metal or opaque bowl to a tray. Glue a watertight cover onto the top of the bowl. The cover will occupy 90 percent of the opening of the bowl. When you pour in the liquid, it will actually go under this cover and into the bottom of the bowl. The cloth has a circular piece of cardboard sewn into its center. Use a regular clear pitcher.

The tray is held by an assistant, bowl in place, cloth to one side, and pitcher—all sitting in a row. Remove the pitcher and fill the bowl. Put the pitcher on your table. Pick up the cloth, without revealing the secret piece of cardboard, and place it over the bowl.

Now for the secret move. Place your hand over the top of the bowl (actually, the cardboard within the cloth) and begin to lift it (the cardboard within the cloth) off the tray. At the same time your assistant will turn the tray away from you, bottom toward the audience. The liquid stays in place due to the cover on the bowl. This cover creates a watertight seal around most of the bowl.

From the audience's point of view, the bowl is under the cloth, held by your hand. The assistant leaves the stage with the tray and the pitcher. The magician walks to stage front and throws the cloth into the air. No bowl, no water, just magic.

This is a simple trick, both to make and to perform. Use your imagination. Try gluing a big glass and a bowl onto the tray. Fill the glass with orange juice and place cereal and milk into the bowl as if you were making yourself breakfast. Use two hands and two cloths. Cover both the glass and the bowl. Then lift them off the tray and toss both up into the air. Hey, it works.

76

CRYSTAL CASKET

With a wave of a wand, you can suddenly fill a glass with all sorts of items.

*T*he magician holds up a small box with clear glass on all sides, showing it completely empty. Then, with a wave of the magician's hand, the box becomes filled with silks, scarves, ribbons, and other items.

THE SECRET:

A fake wall does the trick. It is held in place by a tiny wire catch. All sides of the box, top and bottom, are made from either glass or Plexiglas; the latter is preferred. A good size for the box is five by four by four inches. The lid is on the top of the box.

The fake wall is made of very shiny stainless steel. It is about one inch from the rear of the crystal box. With the stage lights shining upon the box, the fake wall actually looks like glass or Plexiglas. Few will notice that they are unable to see through the box. For this reason, I suggest you do not hold the box or stand directly behind it. If you did this, the audience would not be able to see you or your hand through the box. Rather, let the box remain on the table. Bring the audience's attention to it, open the lid, and stick your hand or wand into the box to show that it is empty.

Close the lid and release the wire catch; once this is done the wall will fall toward the bottom of the box.

It is important to overstuff the section behind the fake wall with ribbons, silks, scarves, and so on. In this way, the various items will put pressure against the fake wall. When the wire catch is released, the pressure of the hidden contents will push the fake wall down and the hidden items will explode into the crystal casket.

77

Dove Pan

Turning fire into a living, chirping bird

*A*nother magical staple is to make birds, rabbits, or other small animals appear. The dove pan (also known as the duck pan, double duck, pan, and double dove pan, etc.) has been around for a long time.

A pan is shown to be empty. The pan is four inches deep, aluminum, without handles. Lighter fluid and flash paper are put into it. After the paper is ignited with a match, a fire burns savagely within the pan. The lid of the pan is placed over the fire, extinguishing it. Just as quickly as the lid closed over the pan, it is removed, and there in place of the fire is a bird, dove, rabbit, or other such small animal.

The secret:

This trick can be purchased at most magic shops. Within the lid of the dove pan is another pan, slightly smaller than the one shown to the audience. It is held in the lid by wire clips. Once the lid with the secretly hidden pan is slipped over the burning pan, the smaller pan is released into the burning pan. The fire is smothered, goes out, and the trick is done. Remove the lid and the animal has appeared.

The animal has been placed within the smaller pan, sealed in the lid from the beginning. Supposedly, no harm can come to the animal since the fire goes out straightaway when the lid removes the oxygen from the flame.

I have always been concerned about the small animal trapped within this and other such devices. I hope that animal rights groups will get involved and stop animals from being used in magic acts: I have heard of too many incidents when a small animal died due to a shoddy magician. I have never used animals in this manner. I have worked with the big cats, but always through trained handlers. The poor pet store animals used by magic acts have no such protection.

78

PENETRATING SALT SHAKER

A salt shaker magically passes through a table.

While sitting at a table the magician announces that he will make a coin disappear. He places a coin on the table; the coin can be inspected. The magician talks about the coin at great length, calling a great deal of attention to it. The magician places a salt shaker over the coin, then a napkin over the shaker. He takes his time covering the shaker. It appears to the audience that the magician might just be taking the coin out in some sneaky fashion.

Just then, the magician looks up and says, "I bet you think the coin is already gone." To prove they are wrong, he picks up the napkin and shaker at one time, revealing that the coin is still on the table. Then, with a quick movement, the magician smashes the napkin and shaker down upon the coin and the table. He hits the table with such force that the napkin flattens out against the table. The salt shaker is gone. It has penetrated the table and has landed on the magician's lap.

THE SECRET:

When you lift the napkin and shaker in order to reveal that the coin is still on the table, you raise your hand up against your lower

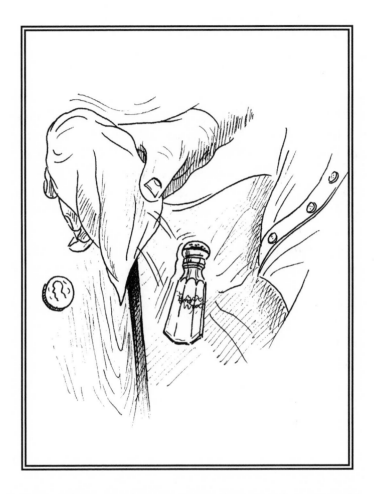

chest area. While all eyes are on the coin, which is on the table, you secretly drop the shaker out of the napkin and onto your lap.

You drop it by releasing a little pressure from your grip. Do not draw attention to the hand with the shaker in it. When you point to the coin with your left hand, secretly drop the shaker onto your lap. Pretend the shaker is still under the napkin and smash it down over the coin (the napkin should retain the shape of the shaker). Reach under the table and display the shaker. "Guess I hit the table a bit hard," you tell the audience.

Another technique is to place the napkin back on the table, over the coin. Some paper napkins will retain the shape of the salt shaker and will be stiff enough to stand on the table. If you use this type of napkin, you could raise your hand and slam it over the napkin, while at the same time opening your knees and letting the shaker fall to the floor; your timing should be perfect. Now it appears that the salt shaker has penetrated the table. If the audience had not been watching the coin, it would have seen you drop the shaker onto your lap when you were displaying the coin.

What about the coin? Well, it never went through the table, so be a sport and leave it there for a tip.

Thanks to Layton MaGuire of Australia for providing the idea for this trick.

79

Pen Through Anything

How to make a pen pierce a piece of paper
without leaving a hole

A regular ballpoint pen is examined, then written with. Then it is shoved through a piece of paper or a dollar bill, anything. The pen can even write once it has the pierced paper attached to it. The pen is removed, with no hole in sight. Great trick. Smart trick, too.

The secret:

The pen is specially constructed. The main portion of the pen is made up of two pieces held in place with a strong magnet. All of this is covered with a thin outer shell.

To make the trick work, start with the pen in the regular writing position. The pen can be given out to be examined, but not TOO closely. Remove the cap and place it on the bottom end of the pen. Now for the secret move: Slide the outer shell down into the cap. This will expose the two sections of the pen, which are being held together with the magnet. The move to push the pen through anything is also tricky, but once you have the pen and you practice a bit, it is a smooth move.

Once the pen has been reunited over the paper, or whatever

you are penetrating with the pen, the magnet holds the two parts of the pen together.

Most of the tricks in this book can be easily constructed. Although I do not doubt that this trick could be crafted in a school metal shop, I highly recommend purchasing this fine trick.

80

POCKET LEVITATION

How to levitate in any location

*T*he magician is out on the sidewalk performing his close-up magic. Suddenly he decides to show his audience that he can float. He removes his jacket and holds it at his waist. He directs your attention to his shoes. Sure enough, in a moment or two his feet and shoes leave the sidewalk as the magician begins to float.

Effectively, this trick will work only in specific and carefully orchestrated environments. The viewing angles on this trick are very unfriendly.

THE SECRET:

Your jacket acts like a curtain, hiding your lower body from the audience. The jacket should extend down to your shoes. Just the toes of your shoes will stick out at the bottom of your jacket. You also need to be wearing shoes that can be slipped off easily. A metal brace is tucked into one shoe, normally the right one. This piece of metal connects your two shoes together. Slip your foot out of your left shoe; the brace hooks this shoe onto your right shoe. While standing on your bare left foot, raise your right foot. Up come the two shoes along the edge of your jacket. It looks like your feet have risen off the ground.

81

NEEDLE THROUGH ARM

How to thread a needle and ribbon through a balloon (or your arm) without bursting the balloon (or hurting yourself)

*T*his trick is used primarily in comedy magic. The magician has a large balloon blown up by a member of the audience. A large, sharp needle is then stuck into the balloon, but the balloon does not break. The needle, with a ribbon through its eye, is then pushed right through the balloon and out the other side. The ribbon, too, is seen to pass through the balloon. Then the balloon is tossed into the air and the same needle pops the balloon.

THE SECRET:

Sometimes it's magic, sometimes it's science, but the illusion must always be given a good performance. You begin with a fifteen-inch-long industrial needle. From the tip of the point, which is very sharp, the diameter of the needle gradually increases to the end.

Use ten- to twelve-inch balloons. The good thick ones are the best. Make sure you do not use too much ribbon, or a type that will bunch up as it passes through the balloon. You might have to experiment with different types.

While a spectator is blowing up the balloon, take the needle and nonchalantly clean it with a cloth. The cloth has been carefully soaked with a household lubricant such as sewing machine oil or WD-40. Get the needle all oiled up. Most people will think you are just cleaning the needle, which you are.

The balloons have a very thick neck and center point. Such balloons can usually be found in most magic and novelty shops. Slowly stick the needle into the thickness of the center point. Then continue to push the needle toward the thick part of the neck, just next to the location where the balloon has been tied off.

The shape of the needle, coupled with the oil, will keep the balloon from bursting and the oil will normally seal the balloon's skin enough so that too much air will not escape. The oil acts as a sealant once the balloon has been punctured. The ribbon, or thread, will simply follow the needle on through the balloon without any harm to the balloon. Then, when you strike the thin midsection of the balloon against the point of the needle: *Bang!* There goes the balloon.

Because this trick depends on science, it might not work every time. You might have a balloon bust on you on occasion, so keep an extra balloon or two onstage when you perform this trick. If the balloon breaks, just try the trick again.

Watch the faces in the audience when you first begin to penetrate the balloon with the needle. People really do get anxious that the balloon will burst.

You can also do this trick with your forearm. Smear a thick layer of clear glue on your forearm. Once it is dry, it will be unnoticeable by the audience. Hold out your forearm and slowly slide the needle under the layer of glue and over your skin. This is dangerous, but if it's done just right the needle will seem to penetrate your forearm.

Complete the forearm trick by pulling the needle all the way through, then use a cloth to wipe off your arm and secretly remove the glue at the same time.

When comedian magician Harry Anderson did this trick, he would squirt a concealed burst of red dye when the needle was entering his arm.

82

FLYING RUBBER BAND

***The magician will make a rubber band fly from his hand and
land on a volunteer's shoulder.***

THE SECRET:

You hold a rubber band in each hand. One is concealed, the
other is shown.

Ask your volunteer to come closer to you. As he does, you put
your hand on his shoulder and leave the concealed rubber band
there. To make sure he and the audience do not notice that you are
leaving the rubber band on his shoulder, you must have the volunteer and the audience concentrate on your other hand, the one with
the other rubber band.

Now take the other rubber band and hold it between your
thumb and forefinger of both hands. Hold it close to your chest
and fold it over in such a way that you have made a form of an X.
With your thumb and forefinger holding the rubber band in this X
position, you can create the illusion that you are holding two rubber bands.

Show this rubber band to the audience. Part the two fingers of
one hand and then the fingers of the other. You are now going to

integrate the two rubber bands into one, using magic. After you show the integration you pretend to follow the flight path of the missing rubber band as it flies from your hand and lands on your volunteer's shoulder.

Kind of a gutsy trick, but it works well—especially in bars and at cocktail parties.

83

REAPPEARANCE OF THE BURNING MATCH

A match is pulled from a pack, is lit, and is allowed to burn.
Then, magically, it reappears, burnt, in the pack.

THE SECRET:

To prepare a pack of matches for this trick, you must take great caution! Bend one of the front matches in the pack forward and close the flap so that the rest of the matches are covered. Light the match using another match. Put the flame out and replace the match in its original position once it has cooled. You are now ready to perform.

Take your pack from your pocket, open the flap with the matches facing you, and use the flap to hide your movement as you pull down the burnt match with your thumb. Still hiding the burnt match with your thumb, ask a volunteer to pull a match from the pack. As he pulls out the match, state aloud that the match came from the place that has your preburnt match. Do not let him check and do not wait for questions to arise. Close the flap, and as you do so, push the hidden match back into place, using the flap to hide your movements.

Turn the volunteer's hand over and place the pack on the back of his hand, strike the match, and vigorously shake your hand to put out the flame. Keep shaking your hand even after you have let the match fly over your shoulder. Keep shaking and tell the audience to watch as you make the match disappear. If you watch your hand so will they. After you make the match disappear, have the volunteer open the pack and find in it the burned match that has not been torn out.

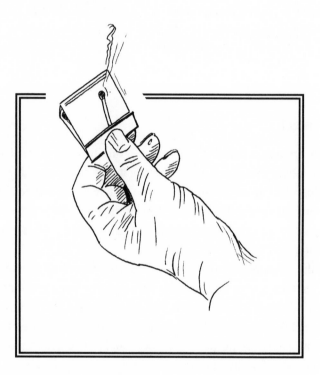

84

CUPS, OLIVES, AND A LEMON

The magician passes olives through solid cups, and leaves his volunteer with a lemon.

*T*he magician has the table set with three cups and several olives. He then proceeds to make the olives magically penetrate the cups. This is done several times. For the finale, a lemon, which completely fills a cup, is produced. To do this trick correctly, the magician will need three cups that can be stacked, a lemon, four olives, and something to use as a magic wand.

THE SECRET:

Place one of the olives in a cup and stack the cups with the one containing the olive on the bottom. Put the other three olives in the top cup. Put the lemon on a chair so your audience cannot see it. You are now ready to begin.

Dump out the three olives from the top cup. Take the bottom cup and flip it over in a fast flowing motion to keep the olive from falling out. Turn over another cup and place one of the olives on top of it. Cover the olive with the third cup and tap all the cups lightly with the magic wand. Lift the single cup and show the audience that the olive is there. While doing so, lift the two cups together and turn them over so that the olive that was put there is now trapped inside the bottom cup. Put the single cup on the top of the pile and flip the bottom cup (with the olive in it) over onto the single olive on the table.

You now have two olives under the cup. Put another olive on top of a cup and cover it with the third cup. Tap the cups with the magic wand and show the audience that there are now two olives under the single cup.

Move the third olive into place as you did with the last two, but now you cover the cup with a volunteer's hand and put the two other cups away. As you do so you pick up the lemon and hold it in your loosely held fist to hide it from view. Tell your volunteer to show the audience that there are three olives under the cup. You take the opportunity to pick up the cup and hold the mouth of the cup in the palm of your hand. Pick up the olives with your other hand and give them to your volunteer. As you do so, tilt your hand so that the lemon falls into the cup. Flip the cup and ask the volunteer how many olives there are under the cup. The answer is not important because when asked to check he will find a lemon.

Some of you might be familiar with the cups and balls trick; this is a simple, more adult version of that age-old trick. The original cups and balls trick is a classic and can be found in most children's magic books.

85

COIN VANISH

A coin that has been placed in a goblet vanishes.

A champagne glass is shown in one hand; a coin is held with a silk in the other. The coin is placed into the glass; the silk is wrapped over the glass and held in place with an elastic band. It is then placed on the table. At the magician's command, the silk is removed and the coin has vanished.

THE SECRET:

This is a simple trick that requires a little practice. The glass is held in the right hand. Hold it by the base in the palm of your hand. The coin is held through the silk in the left hand. In other words, the silk would be draped over your left hand with the coin protruding out or above it.

Turn your left hand over. Now you are holding the coin under the silk. Bring the silk over the glass. When you drop the coin, instead of dropping it into the glass, drop it onto the base and then catch it in your right hand. The audience will hear the glass clink and assume the coin has entered the glass.

Now, quickly cover the glass with the silk, retaining the glass

in your left hand. With your right hand, reach into your pocket for an elastic, leaving the coin behind in your pocket. Seal the silk in place around the glass and place it on the table.

The trick is done; now make the magic happen!

86

THE PITCHER, THE GLASS, AND THE HANDKERCHIEF

***A handkerchief passes through the bottom
of a solid drinking glass.***

*P*lace on the table a tall plastic tumbler (a drinking glass), a cardboard tube, a pitcher of water, and a handkerchief. The glass is filled to the top with water; the water is then poured back into the pitcher. The handkerchief is pushed into the glass, then covered with the tube. Lifting the tube and glass off the table, the magician is able to reach up into the bottom of the tumbler and pull the handkerchief out through the bottom of the glass.

Immediately the tube is removed and the glass is again filled with water, proving that it is solid and that it was magic that allowed the magician to pull the handkerchief through.

THE SECRET:

The glass is a fake; it has a hole about the size of a quarter cut out of one side, near the bottom. When lifting the glass before filling it with water, you cover the hole with your thumb, which will keep the water in the glass. When you pull the handkerchief through the hole, the tube hides it.

87

Dry Water

*A coin is dropped into a bowl of water; the magician
removes the coin without getting wet.*

A bowl of water is placed on the table; several coins are dropped into the bowl. The magician pulls up his or her sleeve and reaches down into the bowl. All coins are gathered up and placed on the table. Audience members are allowed to touch the magician's arm and hand to verify that it is still dry, yet the coins are wet (so is the water!).

THE SECRET:

The water is specially prepared with a

dusting of lycopodium on its surface. This is a chemical available from chemical hobby stores or at some pharmacies. The chemical is both harmless and invisible. What it will do is keep the magician's hand and arm dry when they are dipped into the bowl of water.

88

METAMORPHOSIS

The fastest way to make people appear and disappear

*T*his illusion has been a career-maker for more magicians than any other trick. Perhaps Harry Houdini was the first to become famous for this one, but it was Doug Henning who made his career from it.

A large crate is placed center stage. A group of people from the audience inspect it closely, looking for trapdoors or any other means of escape. Then the committee handcuffs the assistant. Once handcuffed, the assistant is placed into a sack, and the sack's opening is tied over the assistant's head. The committee places the assistant into the crate and closes the lid. Along the lid of the crate, there are several clasps. Padlocks are inserted into them to lock the lid firmly in place. Then the box is wrapped all around with rope and chains; the chains are also locked in place. All the while, the magician is watching the work take place.

Once the work is finished, the group steps back from the crate. The magician picks up a hooped curtain and climbs on top of the crate. The curtain only falls as far as the top of the crate, covering the area from the waist of the magician down to the top of the crate. The illusion is ready to begin. The magician counts "One," then "Two." Each time the magician counts, he brings the curtain up over his head, while the top of the crate is still hidden by the curtain. On the count of three, the curtain drops. Where once the magician stood, on top of the crate, now stands the assistant—a change of place that occurs in only three seconds!

The crate is then untied, unchained, unlocked, then opened. The sack is untied, and inside is the magician, who is handcuffed but now has on a different set of clothes. This is a true metamorphosis, right before the eyes of both the audience and the stage committee.

THE SECRET:

First, the crate is rigged. One side of the top panel opens into the crate. (In some cases a trunk is used, in others it is a packing crate. Either can be employed.) The rigging usually cannot be detected due to creative carpentry. A good carpenter will be able to hide the secret. In addition, most people look for ways to open the crate out, not in. All the chains and rope in the world will not keep the lid from falling inward as it is supposed to, or keep the assistant from climbing out through the chains and rope onto the crate.

Let us begin with the handcuffs. Either they can be the faked type, which the assistant easily opens, or the key can be in the assistant's pocket. No one thinks of this illusion as an escape trick. The sack can be of a gimmicked nature (such as a sack without a bottom), or as the assistant is being tied up, she pokes her hand up into the neck of the sack. This way the rope is tied around both the assistant's hand and the neck of the sack. Remove the hand and the tie becomes loose.

This illusion only seems to require a scant three seconds (the magician's count of "One. Two. Three"). In reality, by the time the crate is locked, then is tied and roped, several minutes have elapsed. The assistant is out of the handcuffs and the bag long before the crate is even secure. Just as soon as the magician gets on top of the crate, the assistant drops open the lid section and crawls out onto the crate. The assistant stays hidden behind the curtain along with the magician.

As the magician counts "One" and "Two," the assistant takes hold of the curtain and the magician drops down into the crate. When the count "Three" is heard, the magician closes the lid and the assistant is revealed to the audience. While the curtain is still in place and the audience is taking in the surprise, the magician makes certain that the lid is back in place. Then the assistant jumps down off the crate and the committee begins undoing it. During this time the magician is changing clothes, putting on the handcuffs, and getting back into the sack. This illusion is a trick that requires a great deal of practice on the part of both the magician and the assistant. When the two of them share the top space of the lid, there is not much room.

When timing the exit onto the lid by the assistant and the dropping of the curtain by the assistant, all movement must be smooth and clean. The change of outfit really makes this illusion sparkle. This effect is especially true when the new costume is clearly different from the first one. This way your audience will not miss the outfit change. This one can be performed inside a theater or out on the street. It is angle-proof and really spectacular when performed correctly.

The crate or trunk should not be too flashy. The less obvious the prop, the more realistic the illusion.

89

THREE-CARD MONTE— JUMBO STAGE VERSION

Make a cougar—or Spot, the family dog—magically appear
from within a triangle consisting of three giant playing cards

*T*hree large cards are brought onstage. Each card is six feet tall and three feet wide. The magician and his two assistants proceed to move the cards about the stage, showing them from the front and the rear. Finally, the cards are moved together to create a giant triangle with a card on each side. The front of the triangle is opened and out pops an assistant with a live cougar. Of course, for those of you who do not have a cougar handy, the family pet will do. Actually, a little sister or brother can even pop out.

THE SECRET:

In the jumbo version, the cougar and extra assistant are always behind one card or the other. The movement of the cards on the stage, the showing of the cards front and back, etc., is orchestrated to keep the cougar hidden.

When the cougar travels from behind one card to the other,

the cards come together just long enough for the assistant and the trainer to move from one card to the other card. This pattern continues until it is time to form the triangle. At this time, the cougar would be behind the frontmost card. The next card forms a point with it, enclosing the cougar. Then the last card brings up the rear, placing the cougar inside the triangle of cards.

This is something you can experiment with using regular-size cards. It is an easy trick to make; you need three six-by-three-foot corrugated plastic sheets. Paint or stick on the appropriate pictures of pips and numbers. In addition, here you have a stage-size magic trick.

90

SUPER CHAIR SUSPENSION

Making a person float over the back of a chair

*T*wo sturdy folding chairs are set up onstage, face-to-face, with a board across the chair backs. A person from the audience is chosen to lie down on the board. She is covered with a large cloth. The chair supporting her feet is removed. Then the board is removed, yet the audience member continues to be suspended in midair. A hoop is passed over her, showing that no strings are attached. Everything is then returned to the original position and the audience member returns to her seat.

THE SECRET:

One chair is a special, reinforced chair with a clamping gimmick on it (this will be explained in more detail in a moment). There is also a gimmick board inside the cloth, that attached to the special chair. Here is the setup: The rear chair (the one supporting the head) is the gimmick chair. It is made with a special brace, and to this chair is attached the gimmick board. The second chair is put into place, then the ungimmicked board.

From the viewpoint of the audience, they see two chairs, a board, and a cloth draping down from the board. The magician then removes the chair supporting the feet. In fact, this chair is not supporting anything. The cloth, which has been used to wrap the audience member, allows a clear view of the board that appears to be floating. Like the first chair, this board has no actual purpose. It is connected to one end of the concealed board and is resting on the gimmicked chair.

The board is removed, the audience now sees a person, wrapped in only a cloth, suspended on the edge of a chair top. Nice-looking trick. The hoop is meaningless, but does add to the effect.

Maximum weight for this trick is about 130 pounds.

At the conclusion of the trick, replace the board, then the chair. Let the cloth hang down off the spectator and take a bow. The entire contraption can be taken down or left for the cleanup at the end of the show. Some magicians actually put the trick together in front of the audience. Others make use of the already prepared chairs as a tabletop for other props during the show. Either way, this is a nice, clean, simple trick.

Once when performing this trick as a headliner at the Steel Pier in New Jersey, I stepped forward to talk to the audience about my next trick while my assistants began to remove the trick behind me. The crowd was not listening to me; they were laughing uncontrollably. Seems that one assistant removed the ungimmicked chair while the other watched helplessly. The joke? The board was still being suspended magically. She put the chair back while the second assistant tried to hide the apparatus.

91

SHADOW BOX APPEARANCE

Using shadows to make people appear and vanish

A framed box sits on a platform. The box is made of one-by-two-inch wood framing with each side of the box lined and formed of paper (or newspaper). The magician shows an empty box by raising the lid and dropping the front of the box. He then closes the box and, to prove that there is nothing tricky going on, an illuminated electric bulb is passed under the platform. Another lamp, attached to a drop-cord, is passed around the box, then put through a hole in the top of the box, where it is left, illuminating the inside of the box. The audience can clearly see the glow of the light from inside of the box. The magic word is spoken, and suddenly a shadow of a person begins to appear in the box. It becomes the complete silhouette shadow of a person. Then this individual bursts out through the paper. You have created life! Well! This is a neat trick—and cheap to build, too.

THE SECRET:

Let's start with the construction. The base is a solid inch or three-quarter-inch-thick board about five and a half or six feet square. Attach to this base four legs with caster wheels on them. The box frame sits on top of this box. The box should be about forty-five inches high and thirty inches square; this will be dependent upon the size of your assistant. The back panel is separate and is hinged vertically in its own middle. One side is permanently attached to the platform; the other side is held in place with pressure. Hiding behind this wall, sitting on the platform, is the magician's assistant, waiting to move into the box.

When you pass the light bulb behind and all around the box, pass it between the assistant and the back panel of the box. Thus your assistant will not be seen but the glow of the light will be seen through the paper. Once you put the lamp into the box, the assistant opens the back panel and slides into the box, closing the panel behind him or her and remaining behind the glow of the light that is hanging inside the box. The audience still cannot see his or her shadow through the paper.

The shadows are created when the assistant inside the box begins to move between the light and the front of the box, casting a shadow on the paper. This should be done slowly and mysteriously. For the finale, the assistant quickly moves completely in front of the light, then tears straight through the front panel of paper.

There are some angle problems with this trick; people on the far sides might be able to see the assistant hiding behind the box. So, if you have such angle problems, do not do this trick. If you must, then make sure you move the trick to stage rear or have stage props blocking the rear view.

I performed this trick on TV and in person for a year or two. It was an inexpensive trick to travel with, since it took up such a small space, yet it played big.

92

SPACE SHUTTLE VANISH

How to make a space shuttle vanish.

*T*he vanishing of one of the NASA space shuttles while it rested on the tarmac at Kennedy Space Center has become one of the most significant disappearances of all time. It was performed before a live television audience while a crowd of onlookers kept an eye on the real thing. It is not an illusion most magicians can afford to perform. Still, I will explain the most common way of performing this trick.

The television audience will see the shuttle as it taxis onto an area of the landing strip. The crew will park the shuttle and disembark. The audience, both viewing at home and on the scene, can see the shuttle from all directions. Spotlights will be pointed at the shuttle, making it fully illuminated against the dark night.

At the magician's command, the lights flash off, then back on. When the lights are turned on, the shuttle is gone. The spotlights are again pointed in the same direction as before, but there is no space shuttle, only the tarmac and the night. The shuttle is then brought back in the same manner. The lights will flash off, then on, and the shuttle reappears. The crew boards the shuttle and taxis it back to the hangar.

THE SECRET:

You will not believe this, but the shuttle never really leaves the tarmac! So how is it made invisible? Seven spotlights surround the shuttle, which is in a cordoned-off area all set for the effect. Between the massive searchlights and the audience, there is a nettinglike substance draped from light to light encircling the shuttle.

When the shuttle is first taxied into the area, it is driven through the one opening between the searchlights that is clear of the netting. Once the engines are shut off and the crew disembarks, the technicians will hook up this last piece of netting. This is done under the cover of preparing these massive searchlights for illumination.

The netting is the same one that is used in stage productions. On the stage, the netting acts as a backdrop for various scenes. With the proper lighting, the scenes will change. For example, when the netting is backlit, you will see an image on the netting; when it is front-lit you will see right through the netting.

In the case of the shuttle, the huge searchlights are set in such a manner that at one point you see through the netting and can easily see the shuttle. In the next light setting, you only see the black of night, since this is the scene secretly painted on the special netting. Black is also the color of the tarmac, so it appears that the shuttle is gone and you see the ground where the shuttle once sat.

When the shuttle is made to reappear, the netting is dropped to the ground while the lights are out. Turn the lights back on and the shuttle has returned.

Positioning of the netting depends on the circumstances. If the audience is only in front of the shuttle, then mask only that part of the shuttle from the audience with the netting. For more angles, use more netting, surrounding the shuttle if necessary. Neither the human eye nor the camera will be able to see through the netting when the correct lighting is in effect.

This netting is only used in stage plays, but many of the modern magicians will use it on their shows and TV specials. It is a great way to make things appear or vanish.

93

THE STAIRCASE

How to enter a box and then disappear

*T*his is not a trick in itself, but is one of the most useful illusions in magic. From Seigfreid and Roy to Lance Burton and every other professional magic magician, the staircase is an invaluable prop. It is simple: a set of stairs on wheels used to climb up into cages, boxes, upper sets, etc. The staircase can be as few as three steps or as many as ten steps. In all cases, it looks like a thin, non-prop, stage apparatus. Nevertheless, the staircase is very deceiving. The steps appear to be quite thin, yet they are hollow and large enough to hold a person inside of them.

An individual will ascend the stairs into an object, let's say a box. The box is covered and the staircase is moved out of the way in order to prove that nothing is below the box (which is up on legs, wheels, etc.). Meanwhile, the person has entered the box, and under cover of the box has slipped through a secret hatch in the box, then through another secret opening in the staircase.

Moving the staircase is not a big deal. In fact, it is moved right off the stage, which no one notices since the attention is on the box. The box is now empty of the person, who has gone into the staircase.

Magic is accomplished with a great deal of misdirection. The magician has misdirected you from watching the real trick: the exit of the person inside the stairs.

You must ask yourself, "Why is that widget up so high that someone needs to use a set of stairs to enter it?" Obviously, it is for these secret stairs! If you want to be a successful magician, you need to use this sort of prop. Once you have built or bought a staircase like this one, you will find many uses for it.

The staircase I use has six steps. It is four feet high, not including two-inch-high caster wheels. On the top, there is a hinged door that opens in. This is the secret opening where you can get in and out of the staircase. The steps are painted red with gold trim. The rest of the staircase is painted jet black. The staircase is two feet wide. The top area is three feet by two feet. The bottom board is four feet by two feet. These are the measurements that work for my set; you can use the right measurements for your own purposes.

The staircase is usually built out of light plywood. The steps need to be reinforced in order to hold the weight of an individual walking up them. The bottom board should be at least three-quarter-inch plywood, for it too must hold the weight of an individual.

94

SHADOW IMAGES

Using a movie projector to project your shadow

*E*lsewhere I talk about shadow boxes. Here is more information on this much-used effect: An enclosure of some sort is seen to have the shadow of the occupant inside of it. The shadow can be seen by the audience on the material that makes up the walls of the enclosure.

In the simplest form, a light source from within the box projects the shadow of the occupant. However, since light bends (see your science teacher for more details), shadows can be very misdirecting. You can experiment with shadows simply by putting a light source behind you and see how you can create shadows on the wall. This is all that is done with a shadow box.

THE SECRET:

This is a more advanced use of a shadow box, mixing movies with the box. In another version in this book, the shadows were created using a light.

Have someone enter the box. Then film this individual moving around in the choreographed manner you wish to project to the audience during your performance. Set up the projector so it will project this film onto a wall of the shadow box. During your show, you climb the special staircase into your shadow box. Slip into the stairs while the movie of your shadow is projected on the wall of the shadow box. The trick is done. You are hidden in the stairs and whisked away to another location while the audience is looking at what they think is you but is only a movie of your shadow being projected.

This type of magic is also very good for television presentations.

95

THE $100,000 MYSTERY

***An empty box is suddenly filled with
five thousand Ping-Pong balls, a rabbit,
and a pail of water.***

*T*his one comes from my good friend and master magician
Burling Hull; he always felt that this trick was worth a great deal
of money to a magician. Therefore, he referred to it as the
$100,000 Mystery. As I was writing this book, I had magician and
magic inventor Andre Kole look at the table of contents. He asked
me if I had meant the Million-Dollar Mystery instead of the
$100,000 Mystery. I told him no. When Mr. Hull invented this
trick, $100,000 was worth a whole lot more than a million dollars
is worth today.

A box that is two feet square rests on a set of aluminum legs
that lifts the box about four feet above the stage. You can clearly
see below and all around the box. In all, the box is about five feet
from the back curtain. Two small doors are on the front of the box.
Open the doors, and the box is empty. Close the doors, open them
again, and five thousand Ping-Pong balls come flooding out all
over the stage.

THE SECRET:

A chute of highly polished chrome, the same diameter as the box, extends from the box, through the back curtain, and into the backstage area. The back curtain itself is made up of a square pattern design. The squares are the same size as the dimensions of the box (two feet by two feet). The highly polished sides of the chute reflect like a mirror. The lighting must be just right in order to reflect the curtain around the chute, hiding the chute from the audience.

The back wall of the box acts as a door between the box and the chute. It is hinged with springs at the top; therefore, anything entering the box from the chute will push the back door open. The springs will cause the door to close once the item has passed through it.

Let us start with simple versions of this trick. Open the doors, and the box is empty. Close the doors, open them again, and a rabbit hops out. Behind the scenes, assistants pushed the rabbit into the chute and through the back door—into the box. Put an empty bucket into the box. Close then reopen the doors, and the bucket is now full of water.

The box is shown empty, the doors are closed, then reopened, and out fall the Ping-Pong balls. The box and the entire chute can be filled with the balls. Pressure from your backstage assistants against the balls, pushing them out, will keep the audience in stitches. Once enough balls have passed the back door, it closes and the balance of the balls falling out will hide the action.

The killer was Hull's finale: The doors are opened and this time a block of wood is seen filling the open space of the box. The magician pulls out the wood and it is revealed to be a long box. He continues to pull, and the box becomes a six-by-two-foot coffin (to make this box look like a coffin, it will need some creative painting). With help from assistants, the magician removes the coffin from the little box (remember, the box is only two feet square). He opens the coffin and out pops an assistant. Behind the scenes, the assistant climbed into the coffin. The coffin was lifted up and pushed into the chute from backstage. When the magician first opens the doors for the audience, the audience sees what appears to be a box. The magician pulls the box, while backstage assistants push the coffin out toward the magician.

96

BLACK ART MAGIC

Make objects appear, float, and vanish

This kind of magic is as close as you can get to real magic and is one of the easiest illusion acts to perform. The magician enters the stage wearing a white outfit, and then slowly the lights go down. The audience sees only the magician because he or she is dressed in white clothing and the stage is now dark. The magician then commands any desired item to appear, float, and then disappear. People, animals, flowers, tables—everything the magician wants—seem to appear, vanish, or float at a command.

The magician goes even further by sawing a woman in half as she stands before the audience. Each half then moves about the stage on its own. Eventually the magician may put the halves back together, or may simply make them vanish.

There is absolutely no end to what the magician can do. In the end, the lights come back up and the magician can either be on-stage alone again, or the stage now can be completely filled with the magical appearances of all the items from the show.

The staging is the main concern. The back curtain or backdrop is flat black. The magician is dressed in white or a very light-colored outfit. The magician should also wear a white mask or have his or her face touched up with white makeup. Hands should be gloved in white or covered in makeup. This will make the magician's hands and face stand out against the black backdrop.

In the dark, with only black light lighting shining on the stage, everything that is black is unseen by the audience. Everything that glows in a black light will be seen by the audience.

THE SECRET:

During the late sixties and early seventies, black light–sensitive posters and art had a great comeback. The poster would seem to shine in the darkness of the black light. Elements not visible in the light of day would become visible once the black lights were shining on them.

To make anything appear, just have your black-clad assistants carry the objects onto the stage. Because the assistants are completely dressed in black, the audience does not see them. Their faces and hands are black, too. The objects they carry will seemingly float onto the stage. On the other hand, you can reach behind the curtain center (where two curtains meet) and produce the objects.

If the object is black on one side and black light–sensitive on the other, you can carry it onto the stage and make it appear and disappear simply by turning it around. People, too, can vanish and appear if they hide behind a cloth of black or a board painted black. Incidentally, adding a strobe light produces an even more amazing effect. The constant flashing light turns the stage into a wave of movement. However, do not keep it on for too long because it can hurt the eyes.

Let your imagination go wild. Forget about traditional magic. You won't need tricks. Just look at your stage as your land of imagination, a place where anything can happen.

To float someone, have an assistant lie down on a black plywood board. Then have two of your black-clad assistants lift the board. The assistant is then floating and can float right off the stage into the wings.

I have had the opportunity to both perform in black light and to see black light performances. It is the most amazing sight to behold, the magic of items appearing and vanishing, objects floating in midair. When you perform black art magic, you can see everything on the stage because you are so close to the action. You might forget how dramatic it all looks to the audience. However, try to keep in mind that black art is truly the most magnificent art form of magic. You will appreciate it more if you have your show videotaped so you, the magician, can review it.

As a television spectacle, black art magic is truly effective, because the set on which you work can be totally dark, while the people at home are in whatever light they choose. Doing black art magic on television is the next best thing to trick photography. The camera sees only what you want it to see.

Black art is truly the cleverest and easiest magic to perform. However, beware: Black art illusions are obviously not meant for close-up acts or for small shows. Moreover, fire regulations can affect how dark you make a theater. You might also have trouble finding a club that is willing to turn the lights so low. One way to alleviate a club's concerns is to have low lighting facing away from the stage area and into the audience. This arrangement will actually enhance the invisibility of the act. However, this illusion, when performed in total darkness, produces effects that are truly eerie.

Black art is labor intensive, but this problem can be overcome by using backdrops that hide your props. The best illusions in black art will have objects or even people float, appear, vanish, then magically move from one place to another place on the other side of the stage. The act can end with the magician slowly vanishing, from the ground up, or simply floating away, off the stage. To vanish from the ground up, an assistant covers the magician with a black mini-curtain.

However you decide to end this act, you must clearly script what you will do and maintain the script. You should follow a story line. You could even use a children's fairy tale as the script. Because the act is in the dark, don't be afraid to talk to the audience during the show. The effect of your voice will be greatly amplified because the stage is black. Your audience will be more focused on what you are saying since they are seeing will be limited. The lessening of one sense heightens another.

97

BOWL OF WATER

One-person version of the Vanishing Bowl of Water
(see page 174)

*T*his was one of my first tricks. It is easy to build, fun to show, and gives the beginner or advanced magician a skit rather than just a trick to perform.

The magician carries a tray with a bowl, a box of magic powder, a clear pitcher filled with milk or colored water, and a scarf. The tray is set onto a table; the liquid from the pitcher is poured into the bowl. The magic power is sprinkled into the bowl, too. The tray, now containing only the bowl and the scarf, is lifted up off the table. The scarf is placed over the bowl. Lift the scarf and bowl off the tray. With a throwing motion, the scarf is tossed toward the audience. The bowl and its contents have vanished.

THE SECRET:

The bowl is glued to the tray. The audience never sees into the bowl; this is a good thing, because the bowl has a top glued to it. This top covers 90 percent of the bowl. The part that is not covered is where the liquid from the pitcher is poured. The scarf has a circle of stiff paper or cardboard sewn into it. The cardboard has the same diameter as the bowl. When you lift the scarf off the tray, you are actually holding on to the circle inside the scarf. As you bring the scarf up off the tray, tilt the tray toward your body. This tilting motion hides the fact that the bowl is still on the tray.

The liquid stays in place because of the lid that covers 90 percent of the bowl's top. Of course, the opening must be at the uppermost area of the bowl lest the liquid drain out when you tilt the tray toward you.

It is a good idea to put the tray down behind something before you toss the make-believe bowl toward the audience. In this way, the evidence is out of sight. Using milk or colored water makes it easier for the audience to see it being poured into the bowl.

98

Flying Carpet

How to make a carpet float; the name is
much grander than the trick.

A person is placed on a carpet. The carpet is held up with swords and a small folding Chinese divider. The divider is removed, and then the swords. Magically, the carpet and the person on top of it continue to remain suspended in air.

The secret:

The carpet is attached to a board; under the board is a metal bar that extends back from the carpet board approximately six inches. The bar bends and then goes down twenty-four inches. At the bottom it bends back in and is attached to a bottom board. The bottom board is similar to the top carpet board, the difference being it has no carpet on it and it has wheels attached to it. The wheels make moving this slightly heavy piece of apparatus around much easier.

The swords are for decoration only. The Chinese divider keeps the twenty-four-inch-long vertical bar hidden during the trick. When the divider is moved back from beneath the carpet, it is moved only as far as the vertical bar extends. The extension is approximately six inches from the rear of the carpet.

From the audience's perspective, removing the swords and moving the divider back gives the appearance that the carpet is floating. Some of the newer versions have the carpet board attached to the bar by means of a rotating coupling. This coupling allows the carpet and its passenger to be rotated a full 180 degrees.

The only thing you can do with the swords is wave them above the head of the passenger and below the carpet in a gesture that seems to prove that no strings are attached.

If you are a creative person, you can build this trick easily if you have access to a metal shop—and cheaply if you have a metal shop do the main work for you. You need a bar that is one-inch square and twenty-four inches long. At each end there is welded another one-inch-square bar that is twelve inches long. It will resemble a large *C* when it is done.

Two pieces of wood are required. Each piece is two-feet square. The top piece is attached to the top of the bar. It is best to attach it with a ball bearing rotation coupling. The bottom or base piece of wood can be attached by drilling holes into the bar and screwing the base to the bar. Ball bearing wheels are fastened on the bottom (base) piece of wood. Paint everything flat black.

Glue a carpet to the top board. If the carpet has a dangling frill, it will help hide the working of the rotating coupling.

The Chinese divider is twenty-two inches high, just high enough to cover the horizontal bar. When it is moved back off the base, it continues to hide the horizontal bar. Cut a notch out of the bottom of the divider so it can sit flat on the floor while resting over the bottom vertical bar.

If you use swords, they can be attached to the carpet by way of magnets. The swords are not needed for the trick, but they do dress it up a bit.

99

BAG OF MONEY

The magician finds a hidden bag filled with money.

*T*his trick gained great fame for the Amazing Kreskin. The magician hands several paper bags (usually five) to members of the audience. Before doing so, he shows the audience that a one-hundred-dollar bill has been inserted into one of the bags. The magician concentrates, then asks the volunteers to set fire to two of the bags and return to their seats with two others. One bag remains onstage. Of course, the hundred-dollar bill is always found to be in the bag left onstage.

THE SECRET:

Again, simplicity is the key to this trick—along with great stage presence and presentation. The hundred-dollar bill is never placed into any of the bags. Instead, the magician pretends to put it in. The money has, in fact, been concealed in the magician's palm during the process of pretending to place the bill in the bag.

At the end of the trick, the magician takes hold of the remaining bag and violently tears it open while the palmed money seems to mysteriously emerge from the torn bag.

I have also seen this effect done in a comedy motif, where the magician will borrow a high-denomination bill from someone in the audience. During the trick, the magician will make out as if the trick has not worked. He does this by tearing open the last bag and pretending to find no money within. Then the magician asks the spectators who helped him before to open their bags, search their pockets, even look under their seats. Still no money. At this point, the audience believes the money has literally gone up in smoke, only to have the magician recover the money from a pocket or behind an ear.

This effect works as above, except the money does not have to be revealed when the onstage bag is opened. A good way to get rid of the palmed money is to reach into a pocket for the matches used in burning the stage bags.

100

WALKING THROUGH A WALL

How to walk through a wall

*Y*ou can do this trick outside or on the stage. The magician invites a large committee from the audience to inspect the wall through which the magician will walk. They will be given full opportunity to rap on the wall, check for hidden openings, and otherwise inspect every aspect of the staging.

The magician will have the committee standing on both sides of the wall, watching every moment of the effect. At the appropriate time, the magician will approach the center of the wall. A group of assistants will assemble a three-part, opaque screen around the magician. The magician will wave his or her hands over the top of the screen for all to see. Just as quickly as the magician's hands go beneath the screen, the assistants completely remove and disassemble the screen. The magician appears to have vanished into the wall. The assistants then will move to the other side of the wall and reassemble the screen. Just as quickly the magician will be seen in the screen, appearing to have walked through the wall. Again the screen is quickly taken apart. Everything can be thoroughly inspected again.

Houdini bought the rights to the original effect in May 1914. Just two months later, Houdini was doing his version in New York City. Many others soon followed with their own versions of this effect. The illusion was a great success everywhere it was performed. I will give the instructions for the most common and practical way of performing this effect.

The secret:

The screen is made up of three sections. Each section is roughly six feet tall and two feet wide. They are made similar to a picture frame, consisting of metal tubing covered with an opaque material. These three pieces need to be able to attach to each other in order to stand up. They are not too much out of the ordinary, but I will discuss them in a moment. The wall, the floor surrounding the wall, everything else involved, is not faked in any way.

The assistants wear workers' smocks, caps, and eyeglasses. All of them appear identical. There are always many assistants when this trick is performed. Not to mention the committee up onstage watching. This crowding effect makes for considerable confusion on the stage and around the wall.

When the screen surrounds the magician, he secretly puts on a smock, eyeglasses, and cap. These items have been hidden in a secret pocket of the screen that was placed around the magician. During the confusion and the movement as the screen is erected, the magician slips out of the side panel and begins to mingle with the other workers, becoming lost in the crowd. Dummy hands, controlled by one of the assistants, are the hands seen waving by the audience. The hands are attached with spring steel wire to the inside of the screen and are controlled by a wire leading to one of the assistants. When the screen is taken apart, the dummy hands are tucked away by one or more of the assistants.

The magician is also part of the team putting the screen back together on the other side. At the right moment, he will slip behind the new screen; remove the cap, smock, and glasses; and then emerge as if he had gone through the wall. Again, the assistants will hide all the disguise paraphernalia as they disassemble the screen.

All of this can be done within a matter of seconds. Timing and teamwork are what is really needed. This type of effect takes great skill and ability. As with any illusion that uses many assistants, practice will make perfect.

This is more like a quick-change act than a magic act. Nevertheless, in the end, it is good showmanship, which has prevailed. Angles must be watched very carefully for this effect to have total impact. Use of lighting for illuminating the screen at the appropriate moment can make the effect actually look as though the magician is disappearing, then reappearing, through the wall.

101

FLOATING ELEPHANT

How to make a ten-ton elephant float

*A*n elephant is walked across the stage, from one side to another. The elephant is brought to a halt at one side of the stage. A screen, just large enough to conceal the elephant, is placed in front of the elephant. Another screen is set up on the other side of the stage. Between the screens are twenty feet of space. The magician makes a magic gesture and the elephant seems to float to the other side of the stage. Both screens are lowered. The elephant has magically reappeared on the other side of the stage.

THE SECRET:

This is a unique trick that was performed at Radio City Music Hall in 1977 during the Guinness on Parade show. The stage at Radio City Music Hall is actually made up of three parts. Each part operates on a lift; in other words, each stage section can be lowered below the stage like an elevator.

For this trick, the elephant, while behind the first screen, is lowered into the understage area on the elevator stage section. The screen hides this. At the same time, the section on the far side of the stage is also lowered. Under the stage, the elephant is walked over to the far-side stage section. Both elevators rise, bringing the elephant up behind the screen on the far side.

In order to further enhance this trick, a spotlight with a silhouette of a flying elephant was shone onto the first screen. Then the spotlight moved up over the screen and was shone against the back curtain. Finally, it came to rest on the second screen, on the far side of the stage. Further distraction occurred when a troupe of dancing girls giggled and danced around the stage to the sound of "flying" music.

This trick was actually called the Vanishing and Reappearing Elephant. The name changed when reporters for *Amusement Business* (a theatrical publication) coined this trick the Flying Elephant. The name stuck, although the elephant never really flew or floated. Only the spotlight, beaming a silhouette of an elephant, flew across the stage.

Funny as it might sound, people who saw the show actually walked out of the theater talking about how the elephant floated! Just goes to show you how strong is the power of suggestion.

Tricks do not have to be expensive or complicated; this trick was created after seeing the stage at Radio City. Look around where you are to perform and see what could be used to create miracles of your own.

102

Orange to an Apple

How to make an orange change into an apple

*T*he magician places an orange into a borrowed hat; he waves his hand over the hat, reaches in, and removes an apple. The orange is gone.

The secret:

Carefully skin the peel off an orange, then wrap the orange peel around an apple. Choose an apple small enough to be completely covered by the orange peel. When the peel dries, it will be stuck to the apple.

Place the specially prepared orange-covered apple into a borrowed hat, reach into the hat, and pull the peel away from the apple.

103

APPLE OR ORANGE

Magician is able to detect the selected fruit.

*A*n apple and an orange are handed to a spectator, one for each
hand. The magician tells the spectator to choose one of the fruits
while the magician's back is toward the spectator. He or she is to
choose the fruit by raising it up over his or her head and holding it
there until the magician says to lower the hand. The magician
turns around and reveals which fruit was chosen.

THE SECRET:

The hand that held the chosen fruit will be whiter than the
other hand. Since it was raised in the air, its veins will be smaller
because the blood was leaving the hand when it was raised.

104

BLOW THROUGH A BOTTLE

The magician blows out a candle through a bottle

*L*ight a candle and set it into a candleholder. Between the candle and the magician, there stands a bottle. Blow toward the bottle and the flame of the candle will be extinguished. It appears as if the magician has blown the candle out by blowing through the bottle.

THE SECRET:

Although the bottle is blocking the candle from the magician, the air currents will flow around the bottle and cause the candle's flame to be blown out.

APPENDIX

Glossary

Apparatus The props used by magicians to perform magic.

Ashra Levitating a covered body.

Assistant The person or people helping the magician.

Black Art Magic performed in the dark, usually with ultraviolet light.

Confederate Person or people in the audience secretly working for the magician.

Force Tricking a spectator into taking the item the magician wants him or her to take.

Gimmick A secret something in a magic trick.

Misdirection The diversion of the audience's attention from one area to another.

Patter What the magician says while he or she performs.

Prestidigitation French word for magic.

Silk Sheer handkerchief, used by magicians, that can be easily rolled into a small ball.

Vanish A person or thing disappears.

FORCING A PLAYING CARD

I have made mention of "forcing" a card in several of the tricks listed in this book. A force is a technique in which the magician makes the spectator choose the card the magician wants chosen. For example, the magician wants the spectator to choose the three of spades. The magician will force the three of spades on the spectator.

Forces found in this book include:

The Mene Teckle Deck.

Although this is not a forcing deck, since you will know which card was chosen by virtue of its double, you will be able to know which card was chosen after the spectator has chosen a card.

How the deck works: As a reminder, the secret to this deck is the fact that it is made up of twenty-six different pairs of cards, for a total of fifty-two cards. Such decks can be purchased at most magic shops. One of the cards in each pair is a millimeter shorter than its mate. The shorter card is on top of the long one. When the cards are riffled, the two cards fall as one. To the audience, it appears to be a regular deck of cards.

The trick: Riffle the deck and have someone insert a finger into the deck, or simply tell you to stop. Cut the cards at this point. Show the top card or have the spectator slip this card off the top of the deck. Once the card has been seen, place it or have it slipped into the deck. Since this card was one of two identical cards, the identical mate remains on the top of the deck after the chosen card has been slipped back in the deck. Pick up the deck, give it a tap, and the chosen card has seemingly moved from within the deck to reappear on the top.

The Svengali Deck.

You will know which card will be chosen since this deck will force the common card each time.

How the deck works: As a reminder, a deck of playing cards is riffled. At a spectator's command, the magician stops the riffle. The deck will be cut at this point, revealing the card chosen by the spectator. While the magician was riffling, it was evident that the deck contained many cards. Once the spectator has seen the chosen card, it is placed on the bottom of the deck. The deck is again riffled; now all the cards have changed into the one chosen by the spectator. The chosen card is removed from the bottom and placed on the top. The deck is riffled again, and now it is back to a normal deck with different cards.

The secret: Every other card is the same. Twenty-six cards are different; twenty-six cards are the same. The twenty-six "same" cards are slightly shorter than the twenty-six other cards. When you riffle in one direction, the short card falls with the long one, revealing the deck as a regular deck. When riffled in the opposite direction, the long cards are held back and the short cards are the only ones seen. The deck appears to be one card.

One Hand Pass.
A standard card force.

Do as I Do.
A little bit of flourish, but a good card force.

Card on the Ceiling—Version Two.
Another good way to force a card in a spectacular fashion.

Behind Your Back.
A simple method of forcing a card.

MAGICAL DATES OF SIGNIFICANCE

January 2, 1905: Magician Maskelyne produces a full-length magic play called *The Coming Race* in London, England.

January 4, 1907: Harry Houdini is chained into a giant football by the University of Pennsylvania football team. It takes Houdini thirty-five minutes to escape.

January 15, 1814: The Great Leitendsdorfer becomes the first magician in recorded history to perform west of the Mississippi.

January 17, 1921: The Sawing Through a Woman illusion premieres on-stage by its inventor, P. T. Selbit.

February 4, 1887: Aki Kuma, the magician who toured vaudeville longer than any other magician, is born in Japan.

February 16, 1903: Edgar Bergman, famous magician and ventriloquist, is born.

March 18, 1734: The first newspaper ad for a magic act is placed by Joseph Broome.

April 1, 1921: The Great Nicola escapes from a straightjacket while suspended upside down over the streets of Natal, South Africa, tying up traffic for thirty minutes.

April 8, 1974: Doug Henning performs free magic shows in parks and on street corners in New York City.

April 9, 1956: BBC-TV, running late in its programming, cut short a television show starring magician Sorcar. The magician was in the middle of his Sawing a Woman in Two trick. Thousands of home viewers believed the woman was murdered and became hysterical.

April 20, 1931: The Great Depression puts an end to the touring show of Howard Thurston.

April 28, 1892: Magician Joseph Dunninger is born in New York.

May 10, 1902: The Society of American Magicians is founded.

May 27, 1957: NBC-TV presents the first ninety-minute television magic special.

May 29, 1783: Benjamin Franklin travels to Paris in order to see an automated, chess-playing, magic machine.

June 5, 1970: Ira Bonewits receives a bachelor's degree in magical studies, an American first.

June 25, 1977: Herbert L. Becker headlines at the Steel Pier in New Jersey.

July 2, 1863: Tad Lincoln, son of President Lincoln, has eggs produced from his mouth by magician Signor Blitz.

July 11, 1849: Magician Harry Kellar is born.

July 20, 1869: Magician Howard Thurston is born in Ohio.

July 26, 1839: The inventor of the Black Art magic, Max Auzinger, is born in Munich, Germany.

August 10, 1836: The first magic shop in America opens.

September 18, 1896: The first movie show in Australia is presented by magician Carl Hertz.

September 19, 1769: George Washington goes to a magic show.

September 27, 1885: Henri Bouton, the magician known as Harry Blackstone, is born.

October 23, 1925: The Great Carsini is born. Most people know him as television host Johnny Carson.

December 20, 1975: Doug Henning performs the Houdini Water Torture Escape on television.

Magic Shops Worldwide

Simply Magic
3767 Forest Lane, Suite 124-1300
Dallas, TX 75244-7100
(214) 358-0397
(800) 206-3817 for orders
Fax: (972) 682-8852
simmagic@flash.net

Louis Tannen, Inc.
24 West 25th St., 2nd Floor
New York, NY 10001
(212) 929-4500
Fax: (212) 929-4565
spinamagic@aol.com

Brad Burt Magic
4204 Convoy St.
San Diego, CA 92111
(619) 571-4749
bburt@magicshop.com

Daytona Magic, Inc.
136 South Beach Street
Daytona Beach, FL 32114
Call us anytime at (904) 252-6767
(800) 34 MAGIC (orders only)

Magie Fantastique
890 BD Raymond
Quebec, PQ
G1C 3L6
(418) 661-2959

Perfect Magic
4429 Kingsway
Burnaby, BC
V5H 2A1
(604) 431-6511

Perfect Magic
4781 Van Horne
Montreal, PQ
H3W 1J1
(514) 738-4176

Magie Spectram Inc
1592 Jean Talon E
Montreal, PQ
H2E 1T1
(514) 376-2312

American Magic Co
136 Doulton St,
St Helens
Merseyside, UK
WA 10-4NZ
Tel: 01744 759653

Camtryx Magic Ltd
187 Gilbert Road,
Cambridge, UK
CB4-3PA

Davenports
7 Charing Cross
Underground Shopping Arcade
The Strand, London
WC2N-4HZ
Tel: 0171 836 0408
Fax: 0171 831 2927

International Magic Studio
89 Clerkenwell Road, London, UK EC1
Tel: 0171 405 7324
Fax: 0171 831 2927

Paul Scott Magic
1 Ashley Close
Penwithick
St Austell, Cornwall
PL26 8UB
Tel: 01726 851823

Presto Magic
9 Brookfields
Stebbing, Dunmow
Essex CM6 3SA

Presto Magic
5701 Atlantic Ave.
Long Beach, CA 90805

Progetto Magia
5 Ashford Court
Ashford Road
Cricklewood, London
NW2 6BN
Tel: 0181 452 7220

Quality Props
11 Hartridge Walk
Allesley Park
Coventry, UK CV5 9LF
Tel: 01203 672512

Repro Magic
46 Queenstown Road
London, UK
SW8 3RY
Tel: 0171 720 6257

Tony Curtis Magic
26 Chillington Street
Maidstone, Kent, UK
ME14 2RT
Tel: 01622 752819
Fax: 01622 752819

Meir Yedid
P.O. Box 2566
Fair Lawn, NJ 07410
Phone: (201) 703-1171
Fax: (201) 703-8872

Hank Lee's Magic Factory
P.O. Box 789
Medford, MA 02155
Tel: (617) 482-8749
Fax: (617) 395-2034
http://magicfact.com

Arjan's Show-Biz Centre
P.O. Box 368
2920 Aj Krimpen A/D Yssel
Holland
Tel +31 180 510011
Fax +31 180 519171

The Magic Shop Copenhagen
Vanmanden 83
3650 Oelstykke
Tel +45) 40 52 38 44
Tel +45) 38 34 35 44

Up Your Sleeve Discount magic
P.O. 610
Friendswood, TX 77549-0610
Tel: (713) 996-5232

Axtell Expressions, Inc.
230 Glencrest Circle
Ventura CA 93003-1305
Tel/Fax: (805) 642-7282

Seattle's Market Magic
Seattle, WA
(800) 903-4271
Fax: (206) 624-4919

Denny & Lee MagicStudio
325 S. Marilyn Aveune
Baltimore, MD 21221
(410) 686-3914

Act One Magic
2727 East 2030
North Layton, UT 84040

Geno Munari's Magic
at the MGM Grand Hotel
3799 Las Vegas Blvd. S.
Las Vegas, NV 89109
(702) 798-4789
Fax: (702) 798-0045

Absolutely Magic
12 Church Street
Bradford, NH 03221
(603) 938-5158

Chattanooga Magic & Fun,
4738G Hwy 58,
Chattanooga, TN 37416
(423) 892-5682,
Fax: (423) 892-1502

Bazar de magia
Casilla de Correo N:161—Suc. 33
(1433) Capital Federal
Argentina
Fax (54-1) 307-2909

The Magic Shop—Copenhagen
Vandmanden 83
3650 Oelstykke

Aladdin's Magic Shop
GPO Box 471, Hobart
Tasmania, Australia 7001
Phone/Fax (03) 62344571

Elmwood Magic & Novelty
507 Elmwood Avenue
Buffalo, NY 14222
(716) 886-JOKE (5653)
(800) 764-2372 Order Line

The Wilder Magic Touring Co.
Matthew Wilder
902 S. Lawe St.
Appleton, WI 54915
(414) 993-5511
(920) 993-5511

Hardini—Quality Magic Items
Postbox 92
D-25828 Toenning
Germany

Magic on the World Wide Web

There are many magic-related sites on the Internet. One of the most popular is the official David Copperfield site, which is maintained by webmaster Todd Cowden. The MagicWeb site is the oldest, most established site on the Internet, having made its debut in 1993.

http://www.magicweb.com: The MagicWeb

http://www.dcopperfield.com: David Copperfield's official site

http://www.alsmagic.com: Al's Magic Shop

http://members.xoom.com/mlgamble: Jonathan's World of Magic

http://www.magicbychaz.com: Chaz

http://www.repromagic.co.uk/club71.html: Club 71 'Zine

http://www.magic.org.za/: College of Magic

http://www.magifest.org/: Columbus Magifest

http://www.magicalmayhem.com/: Mike Giusti

http://www.lvdi.net/~lmoore/hansen/: Geoffrey Hansen

http://www.HoudiniTribute.com/: Houdini Tribute

http://joshuajay.cjb.net: Joshua Jay

http://members.xoom.com/SJMVS/SJMVS/: Steve Johnson

http://www.i-o-f.de/: Industry of Fantasy

http://www.larocksmagic.com: La Rock's Fun & Magic

http://www.MondayNightMagic.com/: Monday Night Magic

http://www.freeyellow.com/members4/ramajik/index.html: Mountain Magic Fest

http://home1.gte.net/pjmoon/PNM.html: Pacific Northwest Magic

http://www.magicrabbit.com/BMagic.html: Ring 69, Bakersfield, CA

http://home1.gte.net/pjmoon/Ring70.html: Ring 70, Tacoma, WA

http://incrediblerohit.8m.com/: Rohit

http://www.magician5.freeserve.co.uk: Kevin Smith

http://home.earthlink.net/~torkova: Torkova

http://hometown.aol.com/wizardspll/page/index.htm: Wizard's Gallery

http://members.eunet.at/jimmybix/default.htm: Jimmy Bix

http://www.sony.inergy.com/crowdgatherer: Dennis Carroll

http://www.lvdi.net/~lmoore/: Michael Close

http://members.aol.com/comedycoll/main.htm: Comedy College

http://homepages.infoseek.com/~magiken1/index.html: Magical Zoo

http://www.hemsleyc.freeserve.co.uk: Emazdad

http://home.att.net/~BallyBoard/: Terry Engen

http://visit.virtualave.net/: Stephan Hochdoerfer

http://www.thehowardfamily.org: Howard DeWayne

http://members.aol.com/Magical33/: Illusions at Large

http://personal.inet.fi/business/markku.purho/jokeri: Jokeri

http://pages.cthome.net/Magician/: Don Kaletsky

http://www.kp-gallery.com/: Kissler Gallery

http://www.krackehl.com/magic/: Jonathan Krackehl

http://members.xoom.com/Magaz/: Magia Argentina

http://clubs.yahoo.com/clubs/magiciansandmentalists: Magic & Mentalists

http://www.magicfunday.com: Magic Funday

http://www.geocities.com/Hollywood/Land/1190/index.html: Magic Hat

http://www.nwi.net/babcock: Magic House of Babcock

http://members.aol.com/antscifi/magic.html: Magician's Knowledge Central

http://members.xoom.com/Magik_Man: Magik Central

http://www.members.tripod.com/cheelman/minky.html: Justin Matlow http://members.xoom.com/XerxX/mental/index.htm: Mental Magic On-line

http://www.inc.com/users/MEPHISTO.html: Mephisto Magic

http://www.dnmagic.com: David Neubauer

http://pages.cthome.net/Magician/nma.htm: New Magicians Association

http://members.aol.com/magic4u01/magic/intro.html: Kyle & Kelly Peron

http://members.tripod.com/~stevep/: Steve Peterson

http://members.aol.com/balloonpop/: Ed Popielarczyk

http://www.rainho.com: Jim Rainho

http://www.ravenmagic.com: Raven Magic

http://www.qcbusiness.com/magicshoppe/: Robert's Magic Shoppe

http://www.angelfire.com/ga/merlindo/index3.html: Paul Sponaugle

http://visit.virtualave.net: Steve's Magic

http://www.psdsi.com/wladimir.magic/: Wladimir's Magic